# KATA JUDO

# KATA JUDO

Demonstration of Throws by T.P. Leggett
Demonstration of Holds by T.P. Leggett
Demonstration of Gentleness
by Dr. Jigoro Kano and T.P. Leggett

Trevor Leggett Adhyatma Yoga Trust

Published in 2022 by Trevor Leggett Adhyatma Yoga Trust

PO Box 362
King's Lynn
PE31 8WQ
United Kingdom

Website address: www.tlayt.org

First published by Foulsham & Co Ltd in 1963

ISBN: 978-1-911467-09-0

# CONTENTS

## THE DEMONSTRATION OF HOLDS

## THE DEMONSTRATION OF GENTLENESS

# JAPANESE WORDS

The following is a list of all the Japanese technical terms used in this book. The Japanese words now form an international vocabulary of Judo and the important ones must be learnt. These are in block capitals, and are essential; the rest are put in for completeness.

| | |
|---|---|
| ASHI | *leg* |
| ERI | *lapel* |
| Garami | *winding* |
| Gatame | *see Katame* |
| Gyaku | *reverse – especially doubling a joint back* |
| Ha | *wing* |
| Hadaka | *naked* |
| Hishigi | *crush* |
| Hiza | *knee* |
| Hon | *basic* |
| Jime | *see Shime* |
| JOSEKI | *place of honour* |
| Juji | *cross* |
| Kami | *upper* |
| Kansetsu | *joint* |
| RATA | *formal demonstration* |
| Kata | *(different word) shoulder* |
| Kata | *(different word) single* |
| Katame (or gatame) | *hold* |
| Kesa (or gesa) | *scarf* |
| Kiai | *abdominal control to help physical and mental co-ordination – often accompanied by a little shout* |
| Kuzure | *loosened* |
| KYOSHI | *kneeling position characteristic of Kata* |
| MAIRI | *signal of submission – light beat against mat or body* |

| | |
|---|---|
| Okuri | *'sending' – there is a technical Judo meaning* |
| OSAEKOMI | *holding down securely* |
| RANDORI | *free practice* |
| Shiho | *four-quarters* |
| SHIME | |
| (or jime) | *pressure on neck causing submission* |
| Shizenhontai | *upright posture, feet level* |
| Shizentai | *(right or left) upright posture, with right or left foot advanced* |
| Tomoe | *a Judo throw in which attacker falls to the ground and pitches opponent over him* |
| TORI | *executant of a Judo technique* |
| Ude | *arm* |
| UKE | *one caught by a Judo technique* |
| WAZA | *technique* |
| Yoko | *side* |

# FOREWORD BY THE TRUSTEES

The Trustees of the Trevor Leggett Adhyatma Yoga Trust are delighted to publish Trevor Leggett's book 'Kata Judo' in new soft back printed and E-book editions. 'Championship Judo' ( with Kisaburo Watanabe) was republished in December 2021 and, with 'Kata Judo' and 'Spirit of Budo' also back in print, all of Trevor's books on Judo are now available once again for all those interested.

The three books comprising 'Kata Judo' were originally published separately in 1963/4 as 'The Demonstration of Throws', 'The Demonstration of Holds' and 'The Demonstration of Gentleness' (with Dr Jigoro Kano) and all three were combined in one volume as 'Kata Judo' published in 1982 by W. Foulsham& Co Ltd.

This new edition of 'Kata Judo' reproduces exactly the 1982 text and readers should be aware that no attempt has been made to update the text for any changes that may have occurred since then.

Trevor Leggett's books on 'Kata Judo' became the Authorised Texts of the British Judo Association on Kata and a Foreword to the 1982 edition was included by the then President, Charles S. Palmer OBE, 8th Dan. Mr Palmer (who was 10th Dan when he died in 2001) said in his Foreword, 'These books have been drawn together into the very concise and clear volume of pictorial and verbal descriptions of how to perform the Katas. It also provides a fascinating glimpse into the history and development of Kata as an integral part of Judo'.

We recognise that the quality of the reproduction of the old photographs do not meet the standards of modern publications but they include photographs of some of the great names in the history of Judo practicing Kata, not least those of Dr Jigoro Kano, the founder of Judo, demonstrating the Junokata.

We hope that the publication of this new edition of 'Kata Judo' will continue to provide a valuable source of guidance on the practice of Kata and its place in the wider practice of Judo.

The Trustees
The Trevor Leggett Adhyatma Yoga Trust
February 2022

# THE DEMONSTRATION OF THROWS

# INTRODUCTION

Kata or formal demonstration is an important part of Judo training. A prearranged opportunity is given and then the appropriate technique executed. Under these ideal conditions, a far greater degree of perfection is required than when a throw is brought off in the flurry of Randori or free practice.

It is now compulsory for students to prepare themselves for examination in the Kata here described before they can take the 1st Dan (first Black Belt grade) in the British Judo Association, the official Olympic body in this country. This book is designed to help them; by studying the explanations and pictures, it will be possible to master all the main points and most of the fine points as well.

I introduce each throw with the formal 'standard' text, as laid down by the Japanese Convention on Kata held in 1960. This text can be taken to be the official version of Kodokan Kata all over the world. Alongside the text are simplified drawings to show the main points. For these I am grateful to Mr. T. Broadbent (1st Dan). It helps to look first at a drawing where only the essential lines are shown; photographs can confuse by too much detail.

The pictures in the strips were taken with a new type of Japanese camera developed for analysis of movement – in general a better picture is obtained than with stills from a ciné film. The demonstrations were made specially for this book by Mr. Kisaburo Watanabe (5th Dan), winner of the Asian Games Judo tourney in 1958, former Tokyo champion, and a celebrated Judo stylist, and Mr. John Newman (4th Dan) who trained for four years in the famous Judo centre at Tenri, Japan.

For further study, especially of the thrower's part, I include some pictures of Mr. Teizo Kawamura (7th Dan); Mr. Kawamura is a noted authority, and fine points can be studied in these pictures. Some other pictures include demonstrations by Mr. Yoshizo Matsumoto, also a leading authority on Kata.

Lastly, to give an idea of the actual movement, on the top right-hand corner and the bottom right-hand corner of this book you will find two typical throws demonstrated in 'flicker' fashion. The pictures begin at the end of the book; hold the pages in the left hand and riffle them down, watching the pictures. They are set out in this way so that you will be looking at a flat surface. These are ciné film pictures and not all the details are clear, but they are put in to give an idea of two typical techniques as they appear when Kata is demonstrated. Once you have the idea of the rhythm of the movement, you can apply it to the other throws.

Study the *text* for details, and the *pictures* for the general "feel" of all the throws. The pictures are not poses but taken at full speed; the occasional loss of clarity is more than compensated by having pictures of what actually happens in real Kata performance.

I have divided the text so that each 'role' is presented in its own column; this makes it easier to learn and check the details.

*Historical*

Before the Meiji Restoration (1868), much of the training in Jujutsu schools was by means of Kata. However certain of the main schools, especially Yoshin-ryu but also Kito-ryu, Tenshin-shinyo-ryu and others had begun to emphasize Randori as well, though not a few still concentrated on Kata alone. Some of the Katas were very long; in the Tenshin-shinyo-ryu there were some 120 techniques.

Dr. Kano in his Kodokan Judo laid the stress on Randori, with Kata as an auxiliary, but this does not mean the latter is ignored in his system. His programme was to teach Randori first, giving instruction as appropriate, introducing the pupils naturally to the principles behind the various waza. After some progress had been made, the Kata training was begun. Dr. Kano compared his training method to learning a foreign language: grammar is at the beginning just taught as points come up in conversation or writing, and only later studied formally. (It may be added that Dr. Kano had a good mastery of English; he was also a leading figure in Japanese education, whose level was and is very high indeed. So he had deep knowledge and wide experience of problems of teaching both in and outside the Judo movement.)

He gave great thought to the construction of Katas for his Judo. Mastery of Kata is necessary, but he believed that the traditional Jujutsu Katas, as they stood, had not much value for his training, and he therefore made a new Nage-no-kata (formal demonstration of throwing) of fifteen throws, and later a Katame-no-kata (formal demonstration of holds) of fifteen holding techniques. In 1908 Dr. Kano took the chair at a big convention of the all-Japan Butokukai (Knightly Arts Association, a semi-official body to which the police etc. belonged, and which had adopted Kodokan Judo in place of the old Jujutsu styles). The convention met to try to formulate a standard system of Kata. At this meeting, which was attended by seventy of the leading experts, Dr. Kano presented the two Katas as then in use at the Kodokan. The meeting unanimously adopted the Nagenokata as it stood, and the other with two or three amendments. These two Katas were to be called the Katas of Randori, as distinct from Kime-no-kata or Kata of extreme measures.

Dr. Kano recommended a book published in 1924 by two of his chief pupils, Mr. Yamashita and Mr. Nagaoka, both of whom attained the rank of 10th Dan. Among the elaborate discussions of each throw are given numerous variations, and in the present book I mention the most important of them.

In 1960 another meeting of prominent Kata authorities was held at the Kodokan under the chairmanship of President Risei Kano (Dr. Kano's son) to standardize the Kata. In this book I have translated the text, published by the Kodokan, of the conclusions reached at the meeting. This text may now be taken as the standard form of the Kata. I include, however, many variations formerly permissible (though not now 'standard') because some of us learnt them and should now reconsider our practice. Most of the details are taken from the Yamashita-Nagaoka treatise, but I have also consulted the later works – none of them, however, so detailed. I studied for some time under Mr. Nagaoka, and some notes are based on his oral instructions.

\* \* \*

In conclusion let me add one thing. Kata is like handwriting. In writing, there are certain accepted forms of the letters, but a good deal of variation is permissible before one can say that a letter no longer corresponds to what it is supposed to be. Similarly in Kata there is a good deal of leeway in performance. But this leeway must not go too far; beyond a certain point the thing becomes definitely 'wrong'. It is better to keep to the original as closely as one can, just as a good writer does, but not so rigidly that the performance becomes stilted and lacks flow.

# JAPANESE WORDS

You need to know the following Japanese words. *Joseki* is the place of honour in the dojo or training hall; in the absence of any other indication, it is the wall opposite the door. *Tori* is the thrower and *Uke* the man thrown. *Shizen-hontai* is an upright posture with the feet level underneath the shoulders; *right Shizentai* is a modification of this, with the right foot half a pace forward and the right shoulder above it. Left Shizentai is the same on the other side. In right (or *left*) *Jigotai* the feet are wider apart and the knees are bent, the shoulders well inside the feet. Often the body is rather bent forward.

*Tsugiashiy* in which many Kata movements are made, is a method of walking in which one foot moves first and then the other foot is brought a half-step behind it. The rear foot never catches up or passes. *Tsuzukiashi* is roughly the ordinary method of walking.

*Waza* means a technique; *Tsukuri* is the preparatory movement, including both action on opponent and adjusting one's own position; *Kake* is the actual execution of the technique. *Tsurikomi* is the lift-pull which is frequenty used to draw the opponent out of balance. *Ukemi* is the Judo method of falling, which is the first thing learnt in Judo and which here is taken for granted.

*Budo* is the collective word for all the knightly arts, including Judo.

# ACKNOWLEDGEMENTS

For instruction in Kata, I owe a debt of gratitude to my first teachers in London, Mr. Y. Tani and Mr. G. Koizumi (now 8th Dan), to Mr. H. Nagaoka (10th Dan) and other teachers at the Kodokan. For help with this book, I am grateful to the members and teachers of the Renshuden, especially Mr. Watanabe and Mr. Newman.

THE AUTHOR

(1982)

*Continuity flicker (No. 18)*

**Bow to Joseki:**
This is done simultaneously by Tori and Uke. In the last picture but one Tori steals a glance to make sure he comes round just as Uke does.

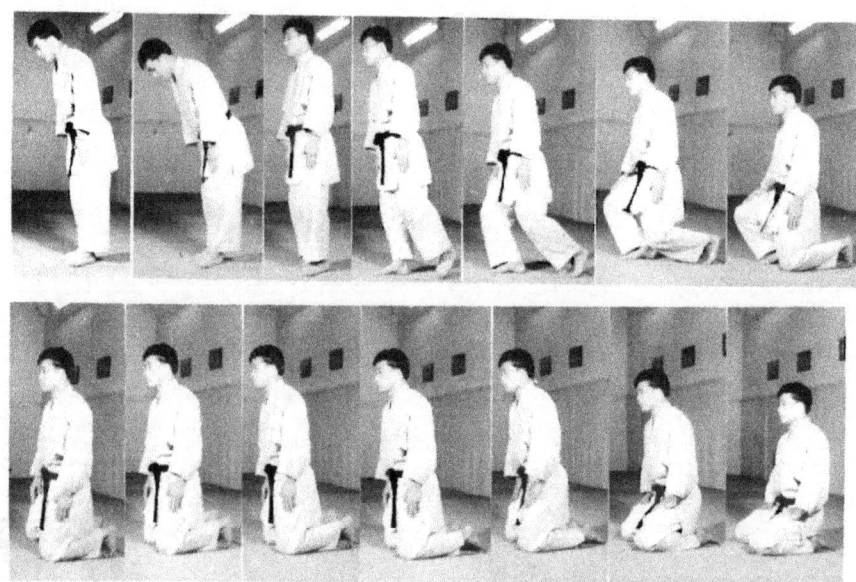

Optional Standing bow, and going down for the formal bow. This must be perfectly synchronized with partner. To rise again, reverse the movements.

# THE PRELIMINARIES

On 10th April, 1960, a national Kata Research Convention was opened under the chairmanship of President Kano. After full discussion, the following was drawn up as a definitive formulation of the Nagenokata.

This Kata is intended as an exposition of the principles of Nagewaza, and three typical throws from each of the five sections Tewaza, Koshiwaza, Ashiwaza, Masutemiwaza, and Yokosutemiwaza are each demonstrated to the right and to the left.

Tori (thrower) and Uke (thrown) take up their places in the dojo, about 18 feet (three mat-lengths) apart, and facing the Joseki. Facing Joseki, Tori is on the left and Uke on the right. They make a standing bow together facing Joseki, then face each other and make the kneeling bow. Rising, they simultaneously take a pace forward with the left foot and then the right, ending up in Shizenhontai (feet level) facing each other. Then they quietly advance towards each other to begin Tewaza.

The demonstration should take place in the centre of the dojo.

For the sake of clarity the movements are here described piecemeal but care must be taken that the movements are not broken up in actual demonstration.

*Notes*

'The demonstration should take place in the centre of the dojo. . . .' This means that in a small dojo Uke only advances one pace to meet Tori. Detailed directions are given in the Notes to each throw. Have a look at the strips on Continuity (pages 18-19) to get an idea how to move from the end of one throw to the opening position of the next throw.

For the bow to Joseki see the strip, and so for the way of getting down and the bow to the opponent.

*Continuity flicker (No. 17)*

**Sitting Bow (za-rei)**
After this, both rise (reversing the previous movements).

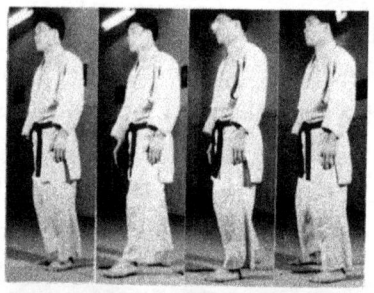

**The Step Out**
Both take a pace forward (left foot, right foot) ending up with feet apart.

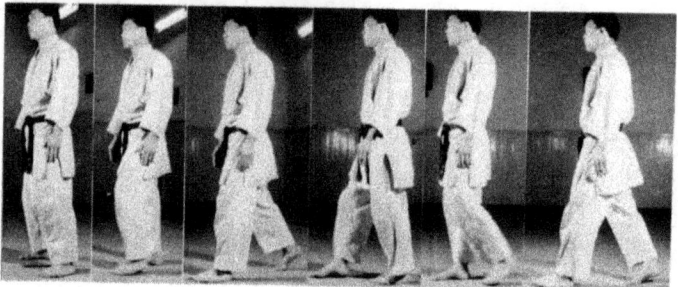

Tori walks across to Uke.

**'The Standard Two Steps' (First Step)** Uke and Tori confront each other.

Uke intends to advance his right foot half a step only and leave his left foot where it is . . .

. . . But Tori, as he takes hold, retreats a full step with his left foot and pulls Uke with his weight; so Uke has to advance a full step with his right foot to keep his balance.

*Ukiotoshi flicker (No.29)*

After the bow, Tori and Uke advance the single step and stop. Note that in the bowing position the feet are very close; with this step into Shizenhontai, the feet come apart till they are under the shoulders. With this step, Tori and Uke look at each other directly.

They are supposed to be in the state of mind called technically Mu-shin, which means literally 'without mind', but can best be rendered as 'without minding'. It is a state of relaxed alertness, fully aware and responsive to outer events, but adapting to them without the inner friction of reactions such as anxiety, anticipation of success, or even the thought 'I am doing this'.

When a Judo man first tries to attain Mu-shin, he either becomes overtense, or else dreamy. The first leads to a sort of momentary cramp in the mind and nerves which checks the appropriate response; when the response is ultimately produced it is wild and over-exaggerated. The second fault means a lax and feeble response without spontaneity. Over-tension is corrected by direct practice of manipulating the mind, especially by concentration on the navel-circle, first in meditation and then in practice itself. Dreaminess is a much more serious fault. An old-fashioned teacher, when he saw somebody practising in a dead way, would suddenly shout or even slap the face, and tell the surprised pupil to be ready to defend himself. After such treatment from an expert the pupil's posture and alertness always markedly improve, for a time at least. It may be that this method of instruction would not be appropriate here, but some means must be adopted to see that Uke especially shows life in his movement. In particular he should not let his gaze roam round the hall as he advances; this always wrecks the look of the Kata.

When first facing each other, and on all subsequent occasions when confronting the opponent in Shizenhontai, both must be careful not to drop into a right (or left) Shizentai, in anticipation of the movement to come.

Advance by sliding the feet, but be careful the knees do not become stiff. When Tori pulls, it is with the whole body, neither rising nor falling. In practice it is extremely difficult to catch the moment just when the opponent advances or transfers his weight, to effect your Tsurikomi; Kata is an opportunity to practise this difficult art, the true secret of Judo throws.

11

*Continuity flicker (No. 16)*

In the 'standard steps' (see the strip) with which many of the throws begin, pull roughly level. Some pull diagonally upwards, but as Uke is already moving this is not in theory necessary. The pull must be smooth.

In every movement, remember to keep the Kata 'alive'; a real master shows poised vitality even in standing quite still.

Study the 'flicker' at the bottom right-hand corner of page 13, and the two 'continuity' strips on the next page, to get the idea of how to move into position for the next throw. Uke has been thrown by Ukiotoshi. Both Tori and Uke keep quite still for a couple of seconds (no more) after the throw. Then Tori rises and moves to the new position; Uke gets up by tucking one leg in and moves round Tori to Shizenhontai, ultimately facing him for the next Ukiotoshi, on the other side.

In the second one, Uke has been thrown by Seoinage, and rises for Kata-guruma.

In general, Tori gets into position and Uke approaches him, calculating the distance. They move, however, more or less together in most cases. Full directions on continuity, together with suggestions for precise positioning for each throw, will be found in the Notes to each throw.

Uke should practise the rolling Ukemi, both rising to the feet and remaining on the ground. In Ukemi, in general, he must remember that it is not now the practice (as it once was) to cross the feet.

*Ukiotoshi flicker (No.28)*

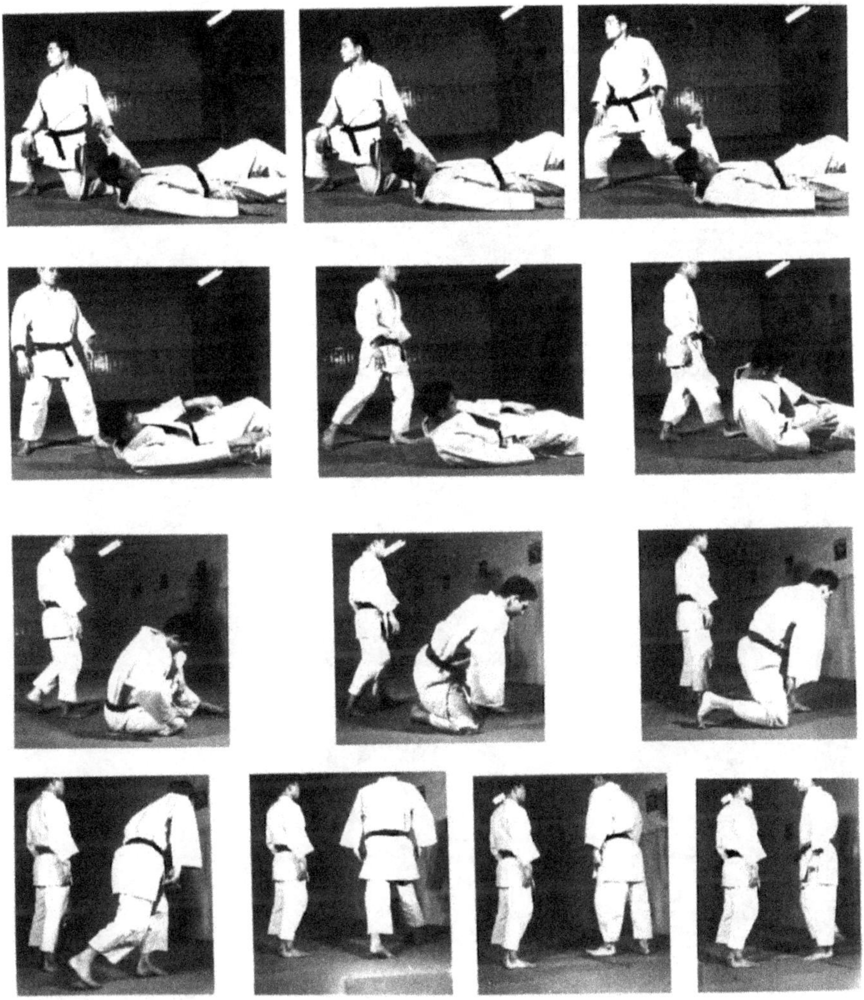

## Continuity (1)

Tori and Uke 'freeze' for a couple of seconds after a throw. Then Tori gets into his new position and Uke comes to face him.

This shows the end of right Ukiotoshi up to the beginning of left Ukiotoshi. The same principles apply to the other throws. As far as possible Uke should face Joseki as he gets up.

Note how he tucks one leg in first, sits up and then stands. The whole movement is briefly described as: "Uke gets up with Joseki on his left."

For Tori's role, see the continuity flicker at the bottom right-hand corner from page 47 backwards to page 13.

*Continuity flicker (No. 15)*

**Continuity (2)**

From end of left Seoinage into position for Kataguruma. Some Toris push the sleeve as shown to help Uke to get moving.

Uke's movement here is described in the text as: "Uke gets up with Joseki on his right."

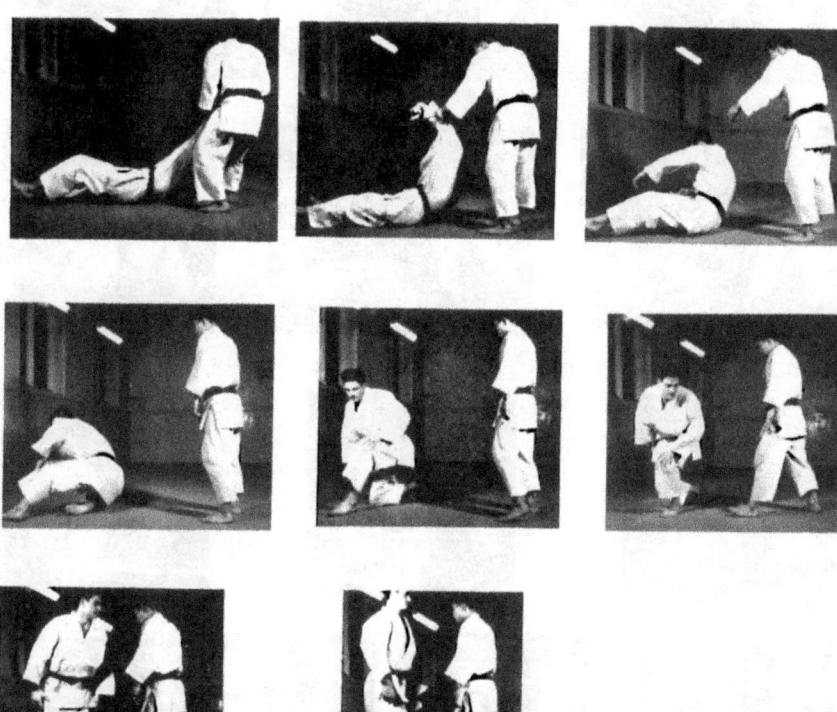

*Ukiotoshi flicker (No.27)*

(1) Tori has walked across to Uke, who comes forward only a trifle.

(2) Uke grasps in right Shizentai and advances his right foot half a step, but Tori steps back and pulls, so Uke has to advance a full step. Tori and Uke here complete the step by drawing up the rear foot. The feet do not come quite together.

(3) (4) Tori again pulls Uke out in the same way.

(5) Tori begins a much longer step, but Uke steps as before . . .

(6) Tori's foot goes right back, and he increases the length of the pull by going down on to one knee. Uke is pulled right over.

(7) Tori must preserve posture; both 'freeze' for a second.

(8) Tori has risen and walked to a corresponding position on the other side to begin left Ukiotoshi. Uke has walked round to face him.

(9) The throw to let follows. At the end Tori rises and stands somewhere near the centre; Uke walks round to face him about 6 feet away.

15

*Continuity flicker (No. 14)*

# GROUP ONE    TE-WAZA
## (Hand Techniques)

### 1. Uki-otoshi (Floating Drop)

Tori and Uke approach to face each other at a distance of about 2 feet.

| Uke | Tori |
|---|---|
| 1. Uke advances his right foot and makes to hold Tori in right Shizentai. | |

| Uke | Tori |
|---|---|
| | Tori takes this opportunity and retreats a step in Tsugiashi (left foot, right foot) holding in right Shizentai and pulling Uke out to unbalance him to the front. |
| To keep balance, Uke yields to the pull and completes his step in Tsugiashi (right foot, left foot). | |
| | 2. Tori again retreats as before, pulling Uke to unbalance him to the front. |
| To keep balance, Uke advances as before. | |
| | 3. Tori pulls again, moving his left foot back . . . |
| . . . Uke advances his right foot a step as before. . . . | |
| | **Ukiotoshi (continued)** Tori suddenly takes his left foot far back, going down on to the knee (toes upright) on the line back from the right foot. The angle between Tori's lower left leg and the line back is 30–45 degrees. With one motion he throws Uke forward and down. |
| Uke gets up with Joseki on his left. **(See page 18.)** | Turning, Tori stands up with Joseki on his right. **(See Continuity flicker.)** |

Uke comes to face Tori at the same distance as before, and moving into left Shizentai they perform Ukiotoshi on the left. Tori gets up with Joseki on his left, Uke with it on his right, and they approach for Seoinage.

## Ukiotoshi (*Notes*)

In the case of tall men, the distance between them at the beginning of the sequence will be greater than 2 feet. The arms should be extended but not straight. Pairs must find their own optimum distance; where there is disparity in height, one or other has to compromise (generally the taller man).

In the throwing action, the hands pull to Tori's left hip; there is no sideways twisting action. (See flicker at top right from page 81 backwards to page 11.)

Uke should keep his weight on the bigger toes and not let himself twist so that he comes on to the small toes. Uke goes straight over, and falls with his feet pointing along the line in which he was advancing.

Uke must not bend or break forward, either before or while he is going over. If he remembers to keep his face up he can generally make a satisfactory fall.

Both Tori and Uke keep perfectly still for one or two seconds at the completion of the throw. Then they rise calmly, but being careful not to let the life go out of their movement. They must not adjust clothing or hair, etc.

Uke sits up and gets up carefully and calmly towards Tori. When it is said 'Uke gets up with Joseki on his left' it means that when he has **finished** his rising, walking and turning, he stands with Joseki on his left. See page 13.

After the second throw (Ukiotoshi on the left) Tori and Uke should be in the same relative positions in which they began Ukiotoshi, but farther apart. From this position they go straight into Seoi. Tori stands still, and it is up to Uke to get the distance right before launching his blow for Seoinage.

*Fine Points*

As explained, the principle is that Tori takes the very long step, pulling Uke in the same direction as previously. Tori goes down on his knee in order to carry his weight even farther back. Uke steps forward with the same step which he has used before to keep his balance, but being pulled so much more and *unexpectedly*, he cannot adjust and falls.

Tori's left knee comes down on the line back from the right foot. The pull must be with the whole body. During the throw Tori's left thigh and body must be erect in an upright line, the abdomen kept forward and tense. The left toes must be upright.

There must be a wide angle at Tori's right knee and ankle; his right toes must not come into the air. Tori does not turn his head.

## 2. Seoi-nage (Shoulder Throw)

*Ukiotoshi flicker (No. 26)*

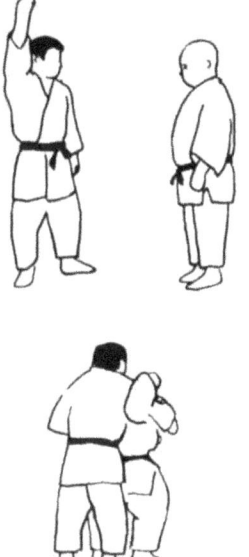

Tori and Uke come to meet each other until there is a distance of about 6 feet (one mat-length) between them.

| Uke | Tori |
|---|---|
| 1. Uke steps forward with his left foot, bringing his right fist over his head; then with a step of the right foot he brings the right side of his fist straight down on top of Tori's head. | 2. Tori deflects Uke's forearm by applying the outer edge of his left forearm, moving his right foot inside Uke's right foot. He grips Uke's right middle sleeve with his left hand and unbalances him forward. He spins on his right toes, thrusts his right arm under Uke's armpit and grips near the shoulder-point, takes his left foot to just inside Uke's left and picks him up, pressed against his own back. |
| Uke gets up and comes to face Tori 6 feet away as before, then steps and strikes with his left fist. | 3. Straightening both knees and bending forward, he throws by pulling down with both hands. Tori stands with Joseki on his right. |
| The throw on the left follows. | Now see page 14. |

19

*Continuity flicker (No. 13)*

(1)  Tori stands about in the centre; Uke places himself about 6 feet away, and aims his blow.

(5)  Tori moves back to the centre; Uke rises and walks to face him about 6 feet away.

(7)  Note that Uke, as in (2), has brought up his left foot in order to come square on to Tori.

(10) Tori stands in the position in which he began Ukiotoshi; Uke walks round him and faces him 2 feet away. (See page 14.)

## Seoinage (*Notes*)

If we take the original three matlengths distance as the 'demonstration space', then Tori can mentally mark out for himself the spot which is the centre. He often finishes the second (*left*) Ukiotoshi about three feet on Uke's side of the centre.

The directions are for Tori and Uke to 'approach each other', but in fact Tori generally stands almost still. If he likes he can get himself on to the centre spot to receive the Seoinage attack. But he must do this while Uke is getting up, otherwise it will throw Uke out. *In all the waza which begin*

*Ukiotoshi flicker (No.25)*

with a blow, it is Uke who adjusts
*the distance, and Tori must stand still* so that Uke gets himself
right.

Uke must be careful to step straight forward with the
right foot and not across. Uke's weight comes between the front and right
front corner, that is, on his middle toes.

The usual thing is for Uke to form his fist as he steps forward with the
left foot; he raises it above his right shoulder at the end of the step. Then
with the right step he brings it over the top down towards the top of Tori's
head. (Tori used to take just one step forward, with the right foot; note that
he now takes two.)

Tori takes the blow on the forearm and carries Uke's arm up and forward,
and he must shoot in as he deflects the blow above his own head. *If Tori
blocks the blow the throw is ruined;* still more, of course, if he pushes back.

After the throw both maintain their posture, 'freezing' for a couple of
seconds with Tori holding the sleeve. Then Uke rises to face Tori and makes
the same attack with the other hand. As always, it is up to Uke to calculate
the proper distance; Tori simply stands still, making sure however that Joseki
is on his right.

*Fine Points*

The whole movement from Uke's initial blow to the final stage of the throw,
is in one unchecked movement; Tori should whip in and throw in the same
breath as it were. To do this he must keep his shoulders soft. If the right
shoulder is hard, it hits Uke's chest and prevents a free turn. Attention
should be more on turning from the hips than centred on the shoulders.
The body turns in one piece, pivoting on the right foot.

Tori keeps the upper part of his body straight as he jumps in, while
bending the knees well. Similarly Uke must not 'break' at the hips; if he
does, this throw becomes very difficult. Tori's hand used to grip Uke's jacket
at the right shoulder; now he is simply directed to grip near
the shoulder point, which can just mean applying the palm
and fingers there. The main point is to secure that there is
no gap between the bodies.

*Continuity flicker (No. 12)*

Tori used to bring his left foot right round inside Uke's left foot, which (unless he moved it) was well to the rear. But now in practice Uke mostly draws up his left foot level with the right, and Tori brings his two feet inside Uke's and throws him straight to the front. If Uke fails to do this, Tori either has to throw him to the left front corner, or run the risk of Uke's slipping off in mid-throw.

For the whole throw, see flicker at bottom right from page 81 backwards to page 11.

**A Randori Seoinage.** In Kata Tori's left hand would hold the inner sleeve.

**Seoi-nage.** Uke should preferably be straighter in posture.

## 3. Kata-guruma (Shoulder Wheel)

*Ukiotoshi flicker(No.24)*

Tori and Uke come together about two feet apart.

| Uke | Tori |
|---|---|
| 1. Uke makes to hold Tori in right Shizentai. | Tori takes this opportunity and retreats a step (left foot, right foot) in Tsugiashi, holding in right Shizentai and pulling Uke out to unbalance him to the front. |
| To keep balance, Uke yields to the pull, and completes his step in Tsugiashi (right foot, left foot). | |
| | 2. Tori retreats in Tsugiashi as before; as he retreats he takes his left hand under Uke's armpit (fingers up) and grips Uke's right middle inner sleeve, pulling to unbalance him to the front. |
| To keep balance, Uke advances as before. | |
| | 3. Tori takes his left foot back in a big step, and pulls Uke so that he steps forward with his right and loses balance. Tori drops his hips into a Jigotai position, and as Uke tips up, applies the right side of his neck to Uke's right hip. He thrusts his right hand not too far through, past Uke's right thigh. Pulling strongly and taking the left elbow towards the hip, he brings his left foot towards the right and stands up in Shizenhontai, bearing Uke up in one movement by the strength of his hips and throwing him to the left front corner. |
| Uke gets up with Joseki on his left. He comes to face Tori and moving into left Shizentai they perform Kata-guruma on the other side. | Tori stands with Joseki on his right. |

*Continuity flicker (No. 11)*

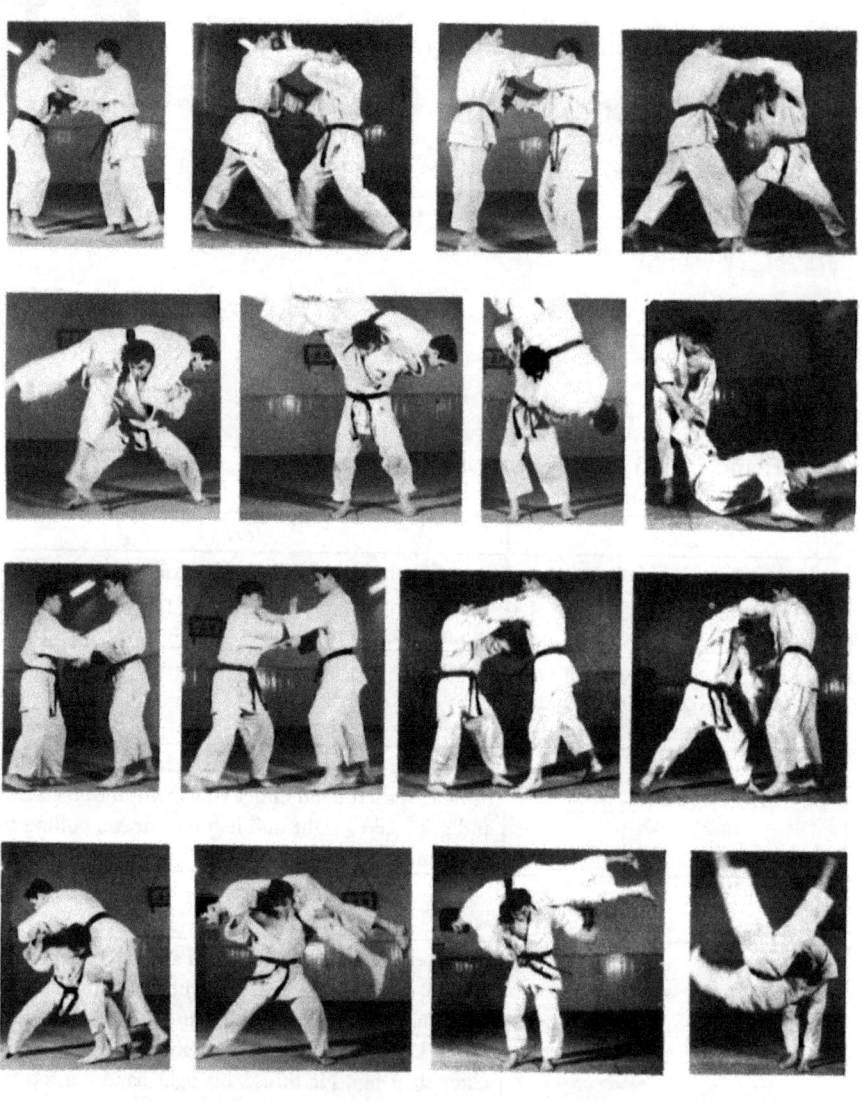

(1)  Tori and Uke face each other. First step as in Ukiotoshi.
(2)  On the second step Tori changes grip.
(3)  End of second step; the feet are rather closer than standard.
(4)  Third step – going in. Tori pulls forward.
(5)  Tori's left hand now pulls down.
(6)  Tori stands up as he draws in his left foot. Uke should arch the back a trifle.
(7)  Tori throws over his left knee.
(9)  Left side.
(10) Beginning the change of grip.

24

Then they both return to their original places, turn to face each other, and quietly come forward for the Koshiwaza section.

## Kataguruma (*Notes*)

After left Seoi, Tori moves to somewhere near the point where he began Ukiotoshi, and waits for Uke to come round in front of him.

Tori changes his grip on step two in order to prevent a necklock when he attempts the throw.

The left hand pull must be continuous and strong, breaking Uke's balance to the right front corner. At the execution of the throw the left elbow comes down towards the hip.

Note that the right foot stays where it is on the third step. Tori steps away with his left foot to get a good pull, and then brings it in again. (In some variations he used to take his right foot out as well, and then shoot it back again, but this is not correct.) Tori drops into Jigotai, and then even lower, which needs special practice for Westerners.

It is usual (though nothing official is said in the books) for Tori and Uke to adjust their clothing, where necessary, before turning to face each other for the new section. This is best done when walking back to the original positions, otherwise there can be an awkward pause.

When Tori and Uke face one another for the next section, they must again look at each other and create the full Kiai alertness and vigour of posture and movement.

### Fine Points

Tori's neck is supposed to come just under Uke's centre of gravity; it is not easy to secure this without bending forward, which is fatal to the lifting action. Tori should feel he is lifting with his right hip.

Uke can help by keeping straight and applying his left abdomen on to Uke's right shoulder. Uke must not bend forward.

Tori does not step out again with the left foot as he throws; this variation is *not* now standard.

*Continuity flicker (No. 10)*

At the end of Kataguruma on the left, both turn the back and return to the original positions. In the old katas the enemy was never to be lost sight of, but in the Nagenokata Dr. Kano relaxed this rule. In fact in Dr. Kano's writings the word 'enemy' does not occur, which is a significant fact.

Tori has been fast here and Uke is, in fact, caught in mid-step of his right foot. Note that Tori's feet come just inside Uke's. The throw is a swing round and Uke goes over all in one piece.

The key picture is the second one which conveys well the feel of the throw.

# GROUP TWO    KOSHI-WAZA
## (Hip Techniques)

## 1. Uki-goshi (Floating Hip)

Tori and Uke come to meet each other until there is a distance of about 6 feet (one mat-length) between them.

| Uke | Tori |
|---|---|
| 1. Uke steps forward with his left foot, at the same time bringing his right fist over his head; then with a step of the right foot he brings the right side of his fist down at Tori's head. | (*the drawings show the action from in front and behind*) |
| | 2. Tori takes this chance and steps in to Uke (left foot, right foot) so that the blow passes behind him. He has lowered his left shoulder and bent slightly back; his left arm goes deeply under Uke's armpit and encircles him round the beltline. Uke is pulled tightly on to Tori's left hip and unbalanced forwards. |
| | 3. With the right hand Tori takes Uke's left outer middle sleeve, and throws him with one twist of his body to the right. |
| Uke gets up with Joseki on his left and comes to meet Tori; at the same distance as before he raises his left fist and the throw follows on the other side. | Tori stands with Joseki on his right. |

*Continuity flicker (No. 9)*

## Ukigoshi (*Notes*)

In the 'approach', Tori may cover more ground than Uke, to get himself somewhere near the centre of the demonstration space. Uke stops about 6 feet away; he is supposed to estimate the distance he will need.

Tori's left arm runs along the belt and not across it or too high. The flat palm is applied, but the feeling should be that the pressure is with the little finger side. If this action is well performed it brings Uke on to the toes of both feet.

Tori pulls Uke's left arm across his own chest so that Tori's hand comes about level with the nipple.

Tori must shoot in; it is not a measured pair of steps, but the feet are moving together. He must be careful not to bend forward, but drop his left shoulder and open his chest. Tori must be sure to get his right foot well turned round, or he cannot make the final twist.

Note that most people feel awkward when making the left-hand blow, and it needs extra practice.

### Fine Points

In Ukigoshi the knees are not forcibly straightened as in Seoinage, but the throw is a simple twist of the upper body and hips. Uke is not lifted but spun about his own left shoulder. In some hip techniques Uke is first lifted and then turned, but in Ukigoshi he is only turned, and the time between getting the hips in and the throw is very short. The throw is thus a fast one. Uke is spun off his toetips to the ground before he has any chance to adapt his posture, and this is the special feature of Ukigoshi.

Uke used to take only one step forward, with the right foot, in this and other throws which begin with a blow. But now he always takes two. The blow is as in Seoinage, down. Some teachers used to discriminate all the blows in Nagenokata, and made this one directed towards the side of the head and not down at the top. The evading movement by Tori was more convincing against this type of blow. In any case Uke, in practice, keeps his weight about evenly between his two feet, and does not come right forward on to the right toes as in Seoi.

## 2. Harai-goshi (Sweeping Hip)

*Ukiotoshi flicker (No.21)*

Tori and Uke come together until they are about 2 feet apart.

| Uke | Tori |
|---|---|
| 1. Uke makes to grasp Tori in right Shizentai. | |
| | Tori takes this opportunity and withdraws in Tsugiashi (left foot, right foot), holding in right Shizentai and pulling Uke out to unbalance him to the front. |
| To keep balance, Uke yields to the pull and completes his step in Tsugiashi (right foot, left foot). | |
| | 2. Tori retreats as before, thrusting his right arm under Uke's armpit and applying the palm to the left shoulder-blade, pulling him forward. |
| To keep balance, Uke comes forward as before. Uke advances his right foot slightly | |
| | 3. Tori swings his left foot round diagonally to the rear of his right, pulls Uke with both hands making him advance his right foot slightly and breaking his balance to his right front. Tori applies his right hip tightly against Uke's abdomen, and throws with a sweeping action as it were, brushing Uke's right leg up with his own right leg. |
| Uke gets up with Joseki on left. | Tori stands with Joseki on his right. |

29

*Continuity flicker (No. 8)*

Uke comes to face Tori at the same distance as before, and adopting left Shizentai they perform Haraigoshi on the other side.

(4) shows the middle of the 'second standard step'.

(5) Tori and Uke have both drawn up the trailing foot, and Tori now begins to swing his left foot round as Uke is about to make the little shift of his right foot which is all he gets of a third step.

(6) Tori begins the sweep up.

(7) Note that Tori's leg is kept straight in the Kata form, and that the sweep takes place at hip level.

## Haraigoshi (*Notes*)

*Ukiotoshi flicker (No.20)*

Tori moves to somewhere near the point from which Ukiotoshi began, and waits for Uke to come round to face him. He does this in Tsurikomigoshi, Sasaetsurikomiashi, Sumigaeshi, Yokogake, and Ukiwaza also.

Tori must not jerk at Uke with his right hand, but use it in harmony with the whole body movement.

Uke's chest must be tightly against Tori's side, at right angles so that the two upper bodies form a 'T'. If Tori turns his back to Uke, as he does in some hip techniques, the final sweep will not be so effective. (Of course Tori's hips do get turned more, but his upper body should be sideways on to Uke's chest; this is the characteristic position of the Kata Haraigoshi.)

Sometimes Tori turns his back, bends forward and bends his right leg at the knee in an effort to get a tremendously high sweep; this is not correct for the Kata, in which Tori's right leg should be quite straight and should rise at most to the horizontal.

Tori's left foot, however, should point in the direction of Uke's advance and not to the right of it, which will lead to loss of balance.

Tori twists Uke as he pulls. The pull of two hands against Uke's upper body is forward and then down, and is supposed to be in roughly the opposite direction to the leg-sweep, which is back and up.

*Fine Points*

In one of the old variations, on the third step Tori used to withdraw his left foot and then his right; then he moved his left foot into position beside Uke's left foot. Now Tori's third step is simply to move his left foot into position. Uke makes a tiny third step – or rather he is trying to make his third step when Tori brushes the leg away.

In Ukiotoshi, Tori made an unexpectedly large third step, so that Uke's full third step was still insufficient. Here he makes not a step back but a diagonal step, surprising Uke by pinning him against Tori and blocking the leg before Uke can make a real step.

Historically this throw was developed when Dr. Kano's pupils began to be able to anticipate his favourite Ukigoshi.

31

*Continuity flicker (No. 7)*

Finally they managed to devise a method of jumping round it, and by practising intensely this method among themselves they were able to escape the Ukigoshi. Dr. Kano absented himself from the dojo for a few days; when he returned he practised with the best pupil at once. The latter, seeing an Ukigoshi coming, essayed to jump round as before, but the teacher extended his leg and caught him in mid-air. This was historically the origin of Haraigoshi, and the succession is preserved in the Kata by demonstrating it after Ukigoshi, and with an Ukigoshi hold – one hand against opponent's back.

(1) Tori comes round into position, keeping a steady pull on Uke's right sleeve.

(2) As Uke shifts his left foot forward, Tori swings round and down into position somewhere above Uke's knees. There is now no preliminary attack at the hip level.

(3) Tori must show good control as Uke is taken over.

# 3. Tsurikomi-goshi
## (Lift-pull Hip)

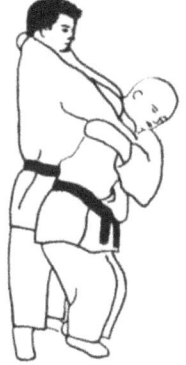

Tori and Uke come together until they are about 2 feet apart.

| Uke | Tori |
|---|---|
| 1. Uke makes to grasp Tori in right Shizentai, as before. | |
| | Tori takes this opportunity and holds Uke in right Shizentai, but with his right hand at the back of the neck holding the collar, and as before retreats a step in Tsugiashi, pulling Uke out. |
| To keep his balance Uke takes a step in Tsugiashi (right foot, left foot). | |
| | 2. Tori again retreats as before, pulling Uke to unbalance him to the front. |
| Uke advances as before, to keep his balance. | |
| | 3. Tori withdraws his left foot a little, pulling Uke out forwards . . . |
| . . . Uke begins to shift his right foot for another step. . . . | |
| | Tori brings his right foot to the inside front of Uke's advancing right foot and with his right hand 'fishes' Uke up and in to him. |
| Uke now tries to preserve balance by stepping forward with his left foot, coming into Shizenhontai with the feet level, and his body tending to brace back. | |

*Continuity flicker (No. 6)*

| Uke | Tori |
|---|---|
| | Fishing Uke out straight forward, Tori swings his left foot round to inside Uke's left, lowers his hips and applies them to Uke's thighs. Then straightening his knees, pushing up with the hips and pulling down with the hands, he throws Uke straight forward with a single motion. |
| Uke gets up with Joseki on his left. | Tori stands with Joseki on his right. |

Uke approaches Tori at the same distance as before, and adopting left Shizentai they perform the throw on the other side.

Then they return to their original positions, turn to face each other, and quietly come forward for the Ashiwaza Section.


## Tsurikomigoshi (*Notes*)

Tori waits for Uke, as explained before.

In the original form of the Kata, Tori used to make a definite attempt to throw by an Ukigoshi type of throw, applying his hips to Uke's abdomen; Uke braced back against this and Tori then made a *second* attempt by bending his knees much more and bringing his hips against Uke's knees. As now standardized, Uke braces himself at the end of his second step in *anticipation* of an Ukigoshi which now Tori does not make; Tori goes straight in for the deep throw.

Uke must keep stiff during the execution of the throw; he must not collapse or bend, but go straight over.

Tori and Uke both used to take a full third step. Now Tori makes a tiny step with his left foot before moving in for the throw; Uke just shifts his right foot, and then as Tori moves in Uke must bring up his left foot level with the right.

Tori's final Tsurikomi has to be carefully studied in this Kata form. His right hand pushes up and forward, and he must be careful to see that his right wrist does not 'break'. Tori's right forearm should come against Uke's left chest or in the centre.

## Fine Points

Tori's left hand pulls straight out to Uke's right side at first; this is to prevent Uke shifting his weight on to his left foot as he brings it forward. Then Tori's left and right hand together pull forward and down in unison as he straightens his knees and pushes with the hips.

Note that the execution of this Kata form is quite different from the most commonly used form in Randori, in which Tori does not push with the hips but tries to pull Uke over the top. In the Kata form there is both push with the hips and pull with the hands.

This throw is to meet the defence to Ukigoshi and Haraigoshi by bracing back; the sequence of the Koshiwaza section of the Nagenokata is an illustration of the development of Judo technique.

*Continuity flicker (No. 5)*

(1)

(2) Tori pushes Uke along with his left (sleeve) grip as soon as he takes hold with it.

(3) End of first step.

(4) Coming to end of second step.

(5) Uke is moving fast and Tori himself takes a big step . . .

(6) Uke's feet were swept away as they came together.

(7) Tori must retain balance at the end.

36

*Ukiotoshi flicker (No. 17)*

# GROUP THREE
# ASHI-WAZA (Leg Techniques)

## 1. Okuri-ashiharai (Sending-foot-sweep)

Uke and Tori approach to about 1 foot distance and stand in Shizenhontai (feet level).

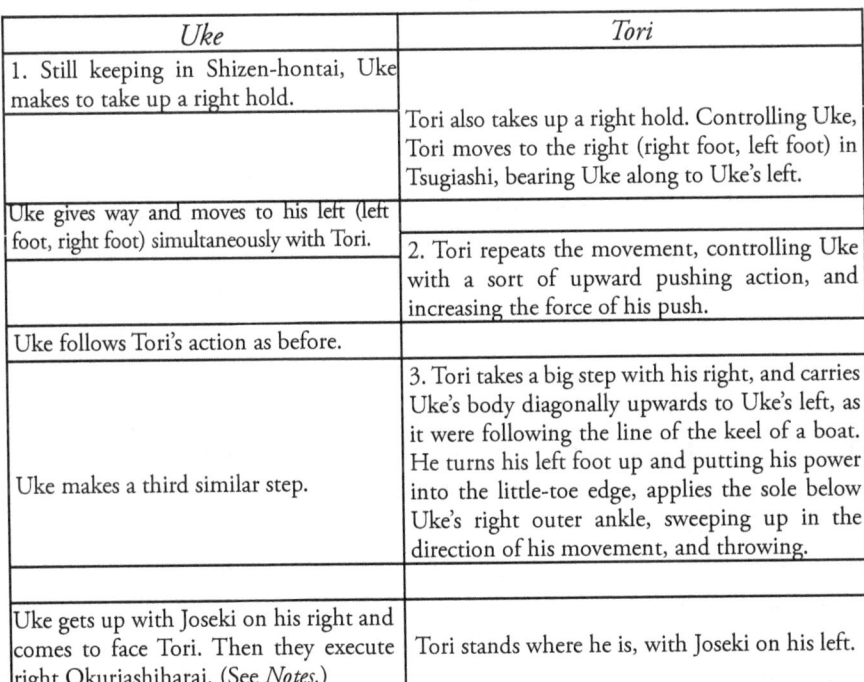

| Uke | Tori |
|---|---|
| 1. Still keeping in Shizen-hontai, Uke makes to take up a right hold. | Tori also takes up a right hold. Controlling Uke, Tori moves to the right (right foot, left foot) in Tsugiashi, bearing Uke along to Uke's left. |
| Uke gives way and moves to his left (left foot, right foot) simultaneously with Tori. | 2. Tori repeats the movement, controlling Uke with a sort of upward pushing action, and increasing the force of his push. |
| Uke follows Tori's action as before. | |
| Uke makes a third similar step. | 3. Tori takes a big step with his right, and carries Uke's body diagonally upwards to Uke's left, as it were following the line of the keel of a boat. He turns his left foot up and putting his power into the little-toe edge, applies the sole below Uke's right outer ankle, sweeping up in the direction of his movement, and throwing. |
| Uke gets up with Joseki on his right and comes to face Tori. Then they execute right Okuriashiharai. (See *Notes.*) | Tori stands where he is, with Joseki on his left. |

*Continuity flicker (No. 4)*

## Okuriashiharai (*Notes*)

The Kata simply states that they 'approach'. In a small dojo they may come somewhat towards Joseki to take up hold, so that the actual throw takes place somewhere in the centre of the mat. In a very small dojo Uke and Tori may take position so that the throw is performed diagonally across the dojo.

Beginners frequently get the grip and direction of the throw confused; remember that Tori's *sleeve* grip brings up the rear. It is with this hold that he finally throws Uke.

The movement should be rapid and smooth, without bobbing up and down, but as if on wheels.

Tori makes his third step with his right foot a big one. Uke makes his third step with his left foot, and is just drawing up the right foot when Tori makes his sweep, carrying both Uke's feet away.

The sweep is made from the hip, and it is a help to make sure the left sole is applied and not the side of the foot. Mechanically it is most efficient to make the point of application as low as possible; a skilful Tori sweeps Uke more or less from the mat level.

The first demonstration, in which the sweep is made with the left foot, is now officially called 'left' Okuriashi, and so the second one becomes 'right' Okuriashi. (See page 42.)

*Fine Points*

Uke used to initiate the move to the side, by making the step himself and trying to pull Tori in the same direction. Now all Uke does is to take up the hold, and as he does so it is Tori who initiates the movement. In practice they move almost together. But the main life comes from Tori, who should be pushing Uke a fraction ahead of himself along the sideways line. Both sides must be careful to keep their feet in line, and not drop into a slight right Shizentai. (However some teachers directed Tori to make his third step slightly in towards Uke, on the principle that for every throw the **ma-ai** or distance between must be reduced.

Tori applies his foot very gently; when the contact is made he increases the force of the sweep. Tori's foot must, of course, travel faster than Uke's foot in order to catch it up, but it should not be so much faster that the sweep turns into a kick. The direction of sweep is exactly the direction in which Uke's foot is already moving, and then slightly upward, following the hands in the latter half of the boat-keel line. This is a shallow curve, something like: ⌣

Note that in this Kata form the hands first carry Uke up before changing to a pull down; in most Randori practice, the hands in Okuriashi go straight down, otherwise opponent can generally twist out of the throw. In the Kata this point is ignored in favour of a very clear demonstration of the principle of the throw.

(1) The beginning of the second step. (Uke is on the left.)

(2) Uke has drawn up the trailing foot and stopped it, but Tori takes his right foot on and out. . .

(3) . . . and before Uke can shift his right foot Tori traps it quickly with his left foot.

(4) Uke goes over in one piece.

## 2. Sasae-tsurikomi-ashi (Supporting Lift-pull Foot)

Tori and Uke approach to about a distance of 2 feet.

| Uke | Tori |
|---|---|
| 1. Uke makes to grasp Tori in right Shizentai, advancing his right foot. | |
| | Tori takes this opportunity and withdraws a step in Tsugiashi (left foot, right foot), holding Uke in right Shizentai and pulling to unbalance him forwards. |
| To keep balance, Uke advances (right foot, left foot) in Tsugiashi. | |
| | 2. Tori retreats as before. |
| Uke advances a step as before . . . | |
| | . . . this time Tori does not bring his right foot to a halt but takes it in a curve along the mat to his right back corner, where he plants it with the toes turned in; he turns his body to the left . . . keeping up the pull. . . . |
| Uke is about to advance his right foot again to restore his balance against Tori's pull. . . . | |
| | Tori applies the sole of his left foot above Uke's right ankle, and on that foot as support pulls Uke over with a big pull of the left hand assisted by the right. Uke is thrown to Tori's left rear corner. |
| Uke gets up with Joseki on his left, then comes in front of Tori. Then they perform Sasae – tsuri-komi – ashi on the other side. | Tori stands where he is with Joseki on his right. |

## Sasae Tsurikomiashi (*Notes*)

Tori waits for Uke in roughly the position at the beginning of Ukiotoshi.

Tori's 'supporting' (left) foot must not push hard, nor of course must it be allowed to fall away; its function is to block Uke's leg from advancing. The action is neither a kick nor a peck; the foot is firmly held against Uke's leg.

The left knee should not be rigidly straight. Mechanically it would be advantageous to have the point of application as low as possible, but in practice that makes the distance too great for control. So the foot is generally placed three to four inches above the ankle on the outside front of Uke's right leg.

Tori should feel slightly bent back at the moment of execution; he must on no account bend forward.

Tori's right foot must be turned a little inwards, otherwise he cannot twist his body for the final throw.

The hands move in one big unfettered sweep. The pull with the left hand is nearly horizontal and in a big curve; at the end it goes down.

### Naming of Throws:

The not very happy Japanese system of naming makes the first Sasae, done with the left foot, a 'left' throw, and the second one a 'right' throw. The same applied to Okuriashi in the preceding section. Ukigoshi, Okuriashi, Sasae, Uranage, Ukiwaza, Yokoguruma are now in the same situation – the 'left' throw is done first. The point is mentioned here because Sasae presents a reasonable convincing case; but it is much harder for a foreigner to see why Uranage should be called a 'left' throw when it comes first in the Kata. However the names have been fixed and nothing is gained by debate. I have given the point some prominence here lest anyone be startled into thinking that there has been some transposition of sides in practice. There has not been; it is purely a question of naming.

### Fine Points

Tori used to take a small third step back with the left and then block Uke's right foot before he could follow. This needed a fast, neat movement. Even now Tori must be quick; he gets the left foot on the opponent's leg almost as his own right foot comes into position. In the interests of speed Tori's third step became smaller and smaller; now he makes no third step at all with his

42

left foot, and does not rest his right
foot at the end of the second step but carries it smoothly
on into position.

*Ukiotoshi flicker (No.15)*

Uke goes over in a complete somersault, and not twisted
round on the right foot. Uke can help by keeping his main
weight on the bigger toes and not letting it get on to the little toes of the
right foot.

The function of Tori's right hand is to keep Uke straight and stretched
out, and also to prevent Uke twisting round out of control. If Uke is not
kept stretched he can easily bring his left foot forward to support himself.
The left hand pulls down only at the end; if it pulls down too soon Uke may
double up and the throw will become awkward.

*Continuity flicker (No. 2)*

## 3. Uchimata (Inner Thigh)

Tori and Uke approach to about 2 foot apart.

| Uke | Tori |
|---|---|
| 1. Uke advances his right foot and holds in right Shizentai. | |
| | Tori similarly advances his right foot and holds in right Shizentai. Now Tori advances his left foot diagonally to the left front, and withdraws his right foot to the left rear, with his right hand giving a big pull to draw Uke round to Tori's right rear corner. |
| Uke follows, moving left foot and then right, in a curve across the mats. | |
| | 2. Tori repeats the same move. |
| Uke to keep his balance, repeats the same move. | |
| | 3. Stepping and pulling Uke right round him to his right rear corner as before, Tori with both hands now breaks Uke's balance straight forward as Uke is just coming on to his left foot. Lowering his own body, he thrusts his right leg between Uke's legs, applies his right back thigh to the inside of Uke's left, and throws by sweeping up. Tori stands with Joseki on his right. |
| Uke comes to face him. | |

Taking left Shizentai, Uchimata is performed on the left.

Both return to their original places, turn to face each other, and come quietly forward for the next group.

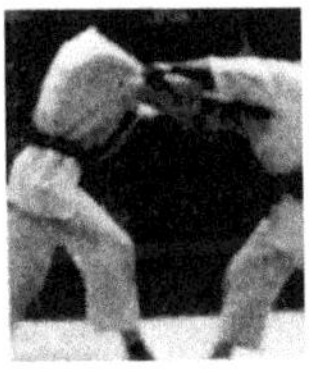

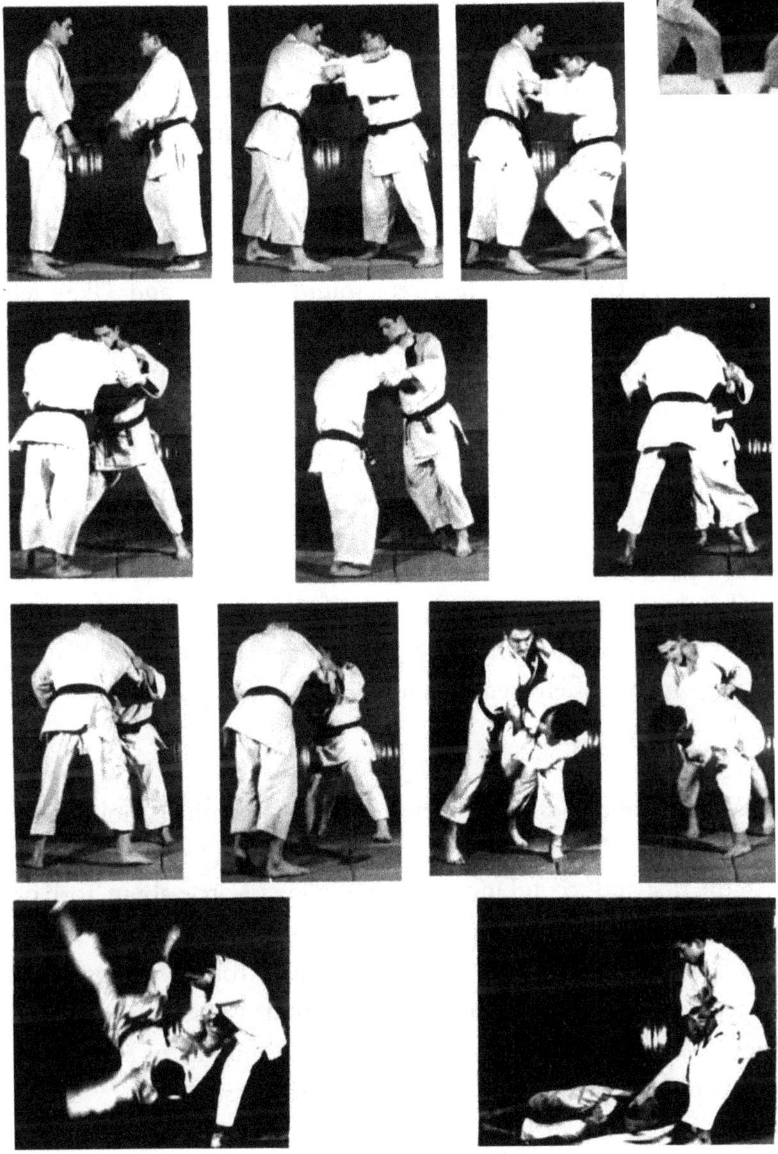

Tori initiates the movement. Uke's legs are swept away from the inside (see Figs. 9 and 10) with something of the action of Okuriashi. This is *not* a hip-throw in Kata.

45

## Uchimata (*Notes*)

This throw is to be done in the middle of the mat, and Tori should wait there.

Some teachers as Tori hold the right hand at neck level.

Tori's big pull with the right hand is about horizontal, and the elbow is somewhat raised. Tori's pull and the steps are one co-ordinated movement; the left foot does move first but there is no halt or gap. The feet must slide over the mats.

Tori pulls Uke almost half-way round a circle, and Uke's left foot, following the pull, nearly completes a semicircle. Both Tori and Uke move the whole body as a unit, not a foot first and then the hips following.

As the thigh sweeps Uke's thigh up, the hands pull in the opposite direction, straight down. Uke comes down inside Tori's left foot.

The throw is in one smooth movement from the first pull to the final Kake. Uke is thrown as he is about to bring his left foot on to the mats for the third step. As he is carried up, his right foot slides across the mats and into the air as in Okuriashibarai.

*This is not the 'springing up' Koshiwaza type of Uchimata* from a static position which is often seen in contest. It is a *moving leg throw*.

## *Fine Points*

As the right foot comes a little forward for the preliminary hold, the left toes turn out a bit.

In the first and second moves, Uke is made to circle about Tori, or about a point just in front of Tori; it is not so correct for Uke and Tori both to revolve about a point midway between them. Tori is supposed to take a *half* step with his left foot and then draw up the right; Uke, pulled by Tori, makes a *much bigger step* with his left. At the middle of step one, Uke is rather behind Tori, and similarly with the second step.

Uke's feet are somewhat wide, and Tori's right foot is nearly in the middle of them at the end of the pulling movement. In practice Uke is made to bend somewhat forward.

The second step, though it starts from a slightly different position, namely with Uke already a bit to the side, is substantially the same as the first and ends in the same position.

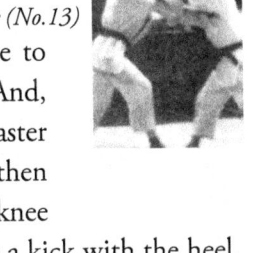

*Ukiotoshi flicker (No.13)*

The sweep action in Uchimata has a resemblance to Okuriashi – it is purely a leg throw in the Kata form. And, for the same reason, the sweeping leg must move faster than the swept leg, and the leg is applied gently and then force is put in. The leg enters with heel first and the knee must be downward. The throwing action must not be a kick with the heel, but a thigh sweep.

Note that Tori does not take his left foot back to the rear (as Randori experts almost instinctively tend to do); but goes a half-step forward to the left front when he is going to make the throw, as in the previous steps.

(1) Uke and Tori engage in Right Shizentai.　(2) Tori pushes and advances with the right foot . . .　(3) Then the left foot, preparing to change grip . . .

(4) On the third step Uke begins to push back.　(5) Tori hangs on to him and drops . . .　(6) Note the action of Tori's hands . . .

(7) . . . ending in the downward pull.

(8–10) Uke rises to his feet and stands quite still for a moment.

# GROUP FOUR    MA-SUTEMI-WAZA
## (Straight Sacrifice Techniques)

In this group, the connecting movements between the waza are speeded up a little.

## 1. Tomoe-nage (Whirl Throw)

Tori and Uke approach to a distance of about 2 feet.

| *Uke* | *Tori* |
|---|---|
| 1. Uke advances his right foot a half step and holds in right Shizentai. | |
| | Tori steps out similarly with his right foot and holds in right Shizentai. Then Tori advances three quick steps, right, left, right, pushing to break Uke's balance backwards. |
| To save his balance, Uke yields to the push and steps back, left, right, left (in step with Tori). Then he begins to resist and push back. | 2. At the instant Uke pushes back, Tori places his left foot inside Uke's right, takes his left hand under Uke's arm to grip the right lapel, and breaks Uke's balance straight forward with a pull of both hands. |
| Uke advances his left foot level with his right. . . . | Tori bends his right knee as much as he can; turning the toes up, he applies them gently to Uke's lower abdomen. He puts his hips on the mat near his left heel, stretches the right leg and pulls in a curve with his hands, throwing Uke over his head. |
| Uke performs right-front Ukemi, ending in standing upright posture. | Tori gets up and stands with Joseki on his right. |
| Uke comes to meet him and they perform left Tomoenage. | |

*Left Seoi flicker (No. 12)*

**Tomoenage** (*Notes*)

Tori and Uke should engage somewhere near the centre of the Kata space.

Note that in this one Tori steps forward with his right foot when he engages in right Shizentai, not backward as in the standard two steps.

Tori and Uke must be careful not to make this forward step too big; it is only a half-step. If it is too big, the subsequent step becomes awkwardly large, because the feet are too widely spaced already.

Tori moves his right foot twice, first the half-pace to take up right Shizentai, and then the same foot to make up a full step. Tori brings his left foot past it (one of the few cases in Kata where the feet pass each other while holding the opponent) for the second, and the right past that for the third. Tori must be careful not to let his body float up so that he gets on to tiptoe.

Uke's steps reflect Tori's; he advances his right foot half a pace for the right Shizentai at the beginning. Then he withdraws his left foot, which is already a half-step in the rear, another half-step to make it a full step behind the right. Uke and Tori move substantially together; it is, however, important to indicate that Tori is *pushing* Uke.

At the end of the third step Uke pushes back, not with the whole body but by bringing his upper body, somewhat bent back from Tori's push, forward again.

Tori must be well in when he throws; otherwise his right leg will tend to push Uke away because he will have to straighten it too soon. On the other hand Tori must not just flop down, slackening or releasing the pull, as nearly always happens when a beginner screws himself up to go right in.

In practice Uke generally advances his right foot just before he takes off, which means it comes beside Tori's left hip. But Uke is supposed to be able to take off from the 'feet level' position.

Uke is now directed to end his Ukemi in the standing position. *This is the only one of all the Sutemi-waza in which he is so directed.* Uke should therefore now stay down at the end of the Ukemi s except for the two Tomoe throws.

*Fine Points*

> 'The horse-chestnut before the flood
>   Throws away its inner self,
> And rides the waves.'

50

This is an ancient Budo verse. Sutemi throws are not recommended to beginners, but Black Belts should make them an important field of study. In fact in the early days of the Kodokan, some of the most important contests were won with Tomoe-nage.

In this Ma-sutemi group, the spaces between the waza are supposed to be shortened; this means that after Tomoe, when Uke has risen to his feet, Tori should get up quickly and be ready for the next throw.

Tori changes his grip at the same time as he steps in – the left foot and left hand move together. Tori changes the grip because in theory if he remains holding the sleeve the grip will be asymmetrical and Uke will tend to be twisted as he goes over. Moreover it brings both hands into the most mechanically advantageous position for leverage, namely as distant as possible from the point of support, the right foot.

Everyone at the beginning pushes too early with the right foot by straightening the knee. Then the hips come too far from the left heel and Uke is merely pushed away. The right leg must be kept well bent. The foot comes just below Uke's navel. The right foot arrives in position just as the hips touch the mat.

Tori's hands move in a curve downwards like this, ↘ but the feeling is of pulling straight downward. Some authorities recommend the whole movement of the hands to be like this: ⊃

Sutemi means to throw away self. Tomoe is the name of a crest shaped like a whirl; one form of it is this ⑤ from which the throw gets its name.

The theory of the throw is that Uke begins to push back with his upper body and Tori utilizes the movement. To make it clear in demonstration there must be no check between Uke's first push back and the execution of the throw in one smooth movement. One moment Tori is standing in front of Uke, and then he seems to disappear and Uke is shot over.

If Tomoe is done really well it gives a tremendous stimulus to the audience, and helps to sustain interest throughout the last two groups, which are often inclined to sag.

*Left Seoi flicker (No. 11)*

Mr. G. Koizumi (8th Dan) executing Okuriashi. This is not a strict Kata form (in which case the sleeve would be held) but the action is very clearly shown.

(1) Uke prepares the stylized blow.

(2) Tori begins his evasive action . . .

(3) Tori must be right against Uke's body.

(4) Tori begins to straighten his knees.

(5) Tori must show the finish of the throw by raising his hips and following Uke with his hands.

## 2. Ura-nage (Rear Throw)

Tori and Uke approach to about 6 feet (one mat-length).

| *Uke* | *Tori* |
|---|---|
| 1. Uke steps forward with his left foot, at the same time bringing his right fist over his head; then as he steps with his right foot he brings the right side of his fist straight down at Tori's head. | (*The left hand drawing is taken from opposite Josekiy in order to show how Tori comes in.*) |
| | 2. Slipping under the fist, Tori thrusts his left foot well behind Uke so that Uke misses and the blow passes across Tori's left shoulder. Tori's hips are dropped and his left arm encircles the back of Uke's hips (belt-line). Holding Uke well in to him, in one movement he takes his right foot inside Uke's right, and applies his right palm, fingers pointing up, to Uke's lower abdomen. With the action of hands and hips, uprooting the opponent as it were, he bends back and throws himself straight back, taking Uke over his left shoulder. |
| Uke gets up with Joseki on the left and goes to meet Tori. | Tori gets up with Joseki on his right. |

They execute Uranage on the other side. (See page 42.)

## Uranage (*Notes*)

Tori waits for the blow well on Uke's side of the centre.

This is one of the most violent Judo throws and special care must be taken. Uke tends to be timid and hang back, and so does not make his blow properly. Then Tori has to force the throw and there is more likely to be an awkward fall. On the other hand, Uke must not simply jump over in the hope of getting his fall in before Tori can pick him up.

Tori must get his left foot well behind Uke as he slips in under the blow. If Tori does not get right in, Uke gets pushed away and the throw has to be forced. Tori must get hips well down, with the feet wide. In the throwing position, Uke's hip rides on Tori's abdomen, and Uke's right leg is between Tori's thighs, one in front and one behind.

The difficult part is when Tori springs up with his hips as Uke goes over. Beginners should not perform this action until Uke has the idea of the fall; Tori can then gradually put it in.

Tori must not hang on with his hands once Uke has passed over. If he does, Uke may suffer a heavy fall. Tori should think of throwing Uke clear.

Uke *remains lying* after this throw, and gets up together with Tori. In conformity with the directions to speed up the connecting movements in this group, Uke should make the second blow straight away with no adjustment of position (which means he must calculate the distance as he gets up).

### Fine Points

Tori used to get more round the back, so that his left hand came right round on to Uke's left abdomen; his right hand was on the right abdomen. There was even a variation in which he put his head behind Uke's back and pitched him forward into nothingness over the right shoulder. This was a most unnerving fall to take. Now Tori is more in front and Uke goes over the left shoulder.

The waza is supposed to flow in an unbroken movement from the original blow. Uke must be tightly against Tori and Tori must manage things so that he does not check Uke's forward action. Nevertheless, Tori is expected to be able to add his own scooping up action to the throw, transmitted through the hands and body contact.

*Seoi flicker (No.10)*

According to the official nomenclature, the throw described is 'left' Uranage, presumably because Uke is thrown over Tori's left shoulder. The point is not important. (See page 42.)

## 3. **Sumigaeshi** (Corner Counter)

Tori and Uke approach to a distance of about 3 feet.

| *Uke* | *Tori* |
|---|---|
| 1. Uke, advancing his right foot, makes to engage in right-locked Jigotai. | Tori adopts a similar right locked Jigotai. |

(In this hold, the right palm is applied to opponent's left shoulder-blade, the right arm passing under his armpit; the left hand is applied to opponent's right upper arm, the left arm trapping opponent's right arm. Opponent's head is on the right side of one's own head; the body is bent forward and the hips a little dropped.)

| | |
|---|---|
| | Tori, floating Uke up with his right hand, takes a big step back with his right foot. |
| Uke yields to the pull and steps forward with his left. After this step, Uke seeks to adjust his position (by bringing his right foot forward again) . . . . <br> . . . to preserve balance, Uke steps forward diagonally to his right front. . . . | 2. (As Uke tends to return to right Jigotai) Tori uses both hands to float him up . . . <br> 3. Just as Uke's feet come level, Tori withdraws his left foot to near the inside of his right foot, and unbalances Uke forward. |
| | Throwing himself straight back, he applies the instep of his right foot to the thigh above the back of Uke's left knee. He springs Uke up from below and with both hands throws |
| Uke *gets up* with Joseki on his left. | himself down and Uke over his head. |

Tori gets up with Joseki on the right.

Uke approaches Tori and they perform the throw from left Jigotai.

Then they both return to their original positions, turn to face each other, and come quietly forward for the next group beginning with Yokogake.

(1) Taking hold.

(2) Hold completed:
the 'locked position'.

(3) End of first step.

(4) End of second
step; the throwing
action has begun.

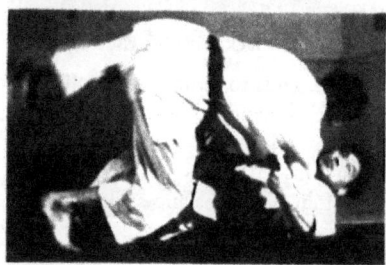

(5) Throwing action: Tori's right foot is
just visible as a dark patch on the inside
of Uke's left leg.

(6) Tori follows Uke
with his hands and eyes.
Uke stays down, and
does not rise as he did in
Tomoenage.

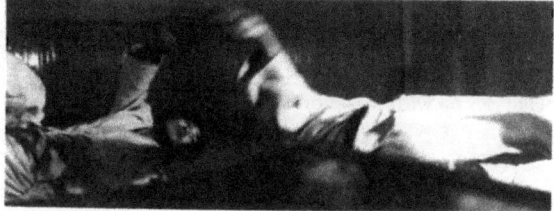

## Sumigaeshi (*Notes*)

Tori waits for Uke in about the Ukiotoshi position.

Tori's first step back must carry his right further to the rear than his left. He pulls with his whole body during this step, the pull being in a curve to Uke's left front corner. Tori's foot travels naturally across in a slight curve. The locked position is maintained throughout.

You often see Tori pulling so hard that Uke stumbles forward and cannot recover; the throw then has to be forced. Uke has to be able to recover from the first pull, and draw himself a little up. Both must keep this point in mind.

On the second step Tori tries to keep Uke 'floating' (though this is more difficult than usual because the left hand, which is the main one, is merely applied to the arm). Tori pulls in his left foot near to his right as he gets Uke to step forward with the right. They both in fact make a bare half-step.

Tori throws himself right underneath, his hips coming by his own left heel. Originally the point of application of the right foot was anywhere on the thigh, but now it is just behind the knee – really the thigh just above that.

Uke is taken over the left side of Tori's head. Care must be taken not to tip Uke over to the side, which would make the throw a Yokosutemi.

Tori must be flat on his back, and the whole throw must be executed in one unbroken pull from the beginning of the second step.

*Uke is not directed to stand up.* Many experts always used to stand up as part of the Ukemi, but now Uke should remain lying down.

It is important that Tori should *show* the body action by keeping his hips slightly raised from the ground during the little pose at the end of the throw. Ideally his left foot should be supported on the toes, which again shows the force of the throwing movement. Tori should look towards Uke at the end of the throw, and keep his hands extended, to make it clear exactly who has made the throw; people who have never seen Judo are sometimes bewildered when they see both men lying on their backs at the end, and wonder who is supposed to have 'won'.

*Fine Points*

Sumigaeshi is not a well-known throw; however, the famous champion Toku (8th Dan),

59

himself some six-foot tall, recommended it to Europeans as a throw with a great future for long-legged men. It is used specially against a rigid defensive attitude, and as such it is shown in the Kata.

Uke's left foot remains on the ground after the right has gone. This is as much as is achieved in most performances of Yokogake; nevertheless, the ideal is that both feet should be carried away at the same moment, though the fall is a heavy one.

The 'locked' Jigotai goes back to the early days of Ju-jutsu. The heads may touch on the right side. Note that it is not correct to grasp the sleeve and belt in this hold, as once was popular.

*Some experts hold the sleeve in order to give Uke an easier fall;* this is not against the spirit of the throw, and is a permissible variation. It helps to avoid the danger of Uke's getting his right arm trapped.

As Uke goes over his face should be turned to the left and his right shoulder brought forward towards Tori's left shoulder. Beginners sometimes tend to face to the right, which can lead to a sticky fall.

# GROUP FIVE    YOKO-SUTEMI-WAZA
## (Side Sacrifice Techniques)

### 1. Yoko-gake (Side Hook)

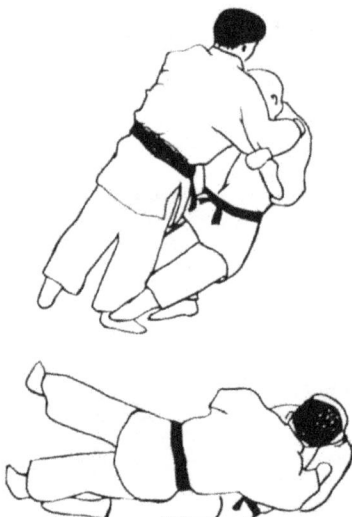

Tori and Uke approach to
a distance of about 2 feet.

| *Uke* | *Tori* |
|---|---|
| 1. Uke advances his right foot and makes to hold in right Shizentai. | Tori takes this opportunity and withdraws a step with the left foot in Tsugiashi (left foot, right foot), holding in right Shizentai and pulling Uke to unbalance him forward. |
| To keep balance, Uke yields and advances in Tsugiashi (right foot, left foot). | |
| | 2. Tori again retreats, pulling Uke . . . |
| Uke again advances in Tsugiashi, but now with his body a bit braced back . . . | 3. Tori takes his left foot back a little . . . |

*Ukiotoshi flicker (No.8)*

| *Uke* | *Tori* |
|---|---|
| | then Tori brings his right foot near his own |
| Uke in the braced-back | left foot, and with the action of both hands |
| posture shifts his right foot | unbalances Uke on to the outer edge of the |
| forward . . . | right foot. Tori throws himself on to his |
| | left side, sweeping with a thrusting action |
| | at the front outside of the part below Uke's |
| | outer ankle; at the same time Tori as it were |
| | scoops up in an arc with his left hand, with |
| | the right hand helping. This throws Uke to |
| | Tori's left side. |
| Uke gets up with Joseki on | Tori gets up with Joseki on his left. |
| his right. | |

Uke approaches Tori and they perform the other Yokogake. (See page 42.)

## Yokogake (*Notes*)

Tori and Uke engage as for Ukiotoshi.

Yokogake is a difficult one to perform well.

Uke stands straight at the end of the second step; his weight is on his right toes, with which he is bracing back. It is best if Uke is more on his little toes, or the outher edge of the foot. Uke must not bend forward or collapse.

Tori makes the sweep with his whole body, also fairly straight. Tori must not sweep and then fall, or try to fall and then sweep; sweep and fall are the same movement – he sweeps as he falls, falls as he sweeps.

Tori's hips must not bend. His left hip should come down not far from where Uke's right foot was planted, or in other words Tori's whole leg shoots right through.

At the end, Tori's left fist is above his left breast. Tori and Uke finish up lying side by side. This is a heavy fall and Tori should take care to keep Uke's head up.

Tori must be on his left side and not on his back. It is best if Tori grips the ground firmly with his right foot and keeps the left leg well outstretched into the air during the short pose at the end of the throw; this makes the throwing movement clear to the spectators. Uke ends up flat on his back, breaking fall with the left hand, and with his legs straight out.

*Left Seoi flicker (No. 8)*

*Fine Points*

In the Masutemi group the interval between the throws was shortened. This meant a speeding up of the Kata; it is important at the beginning of Yokogake to re-establish the original pace.

The hand movement has several refinements. Tori on the second step pulls in slightly with his left hand, and pushes slightly with his right hand across to the left, with the idea of making Uke brace back and a bit to the right.* As a result, Uke's second step is slightly inwards and his body inclined a little back. Tori's change of pull must not be a sharp jerk, but as it would have to be in practice, a gentle pressure to which Uke's body will not react consciously. Uke helps by taking his right shoulder a little in and stepping somewhat inwards with his right foot on the second step.

Tori used to make a full third step back with his left and then, without drawing the right foot up to it, he made the sweep with the left from where he was. This meant he was very much in front of Uke, and the fall was a most awkward one, especially if Tori had not got much twist on to Uke. Now Tori makes a small third step with the left and immediately draws his right foot up to it, which brings him more to Uke's right side when he makes the attack.

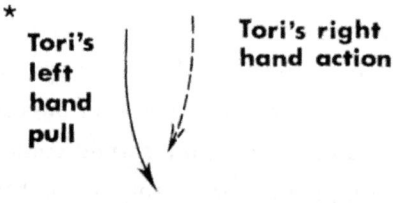

\*

**Tori's left hand pull**    **Tori's right hand action**

## 2. **Yoko-guruma** (Side Wheel)

*(All drawings are from opposite Joseki)*

Tori and Uke approach to about 6 feet distance.

| *Uke* | *Tori* |
|---|---|
| 1. Uke aims a blow at Tori's head as in Uranage. | 2. Tori takes the opportunity and comes in for Uranage. |
| Uke attempts to avoid being thrown by abruptly bending forward the upper part of his body. | 3. Tori utilizes this new position of Uke by pulling him straight forward with the left hand. He slides his right leg in a curve deeply between Uke's legs and throws his own body on to his left side. His right hand pushes somewhat upwards and he throws Uke over the left shoulder. |
| Uke gets up with Joseki on his left. | Tori gets up with Joseki on the right. |

Uke comes to face Tori and they execute the other Yokoguruma. (See page 42.)

The pictures are taken from BEHIND TORI in order to show the action clearly.

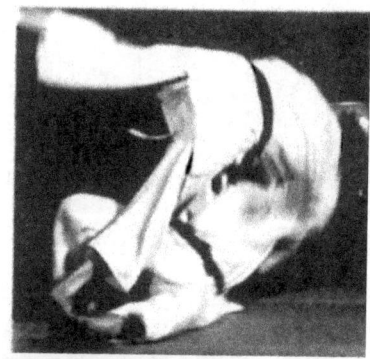

Another picture of the moment of execution. The whirl characteristic of Yokoguruma appears clearly.

## Yokoguruma (*Notes*)

*Ukiotoshi flicker (No. 6)*

Tori waits as for Uranage.

Tori must thrust his right leg deeply through and get his head well down, otherwise he will not be low enough for Uke, in his bent posture, to go over easily. The outside of Tori's right leg slides against the mats, and Tori must come under Uke's centre of gravity. The bodies must be kept locked together throughout.

Tori has to make a big turn to get on to his left side, and Uke is thrown in the direction his head is pointing, i.e. almost at right angles to the line of the original Uranage attempt. Tori should be well on his left side, not on his back as in Uranage; the two throws are quite distinct.

Some teachers say that the power comes from the left foot, and that the right foot does not touch the ground. Others put the toes of the right foot on the ground and allow the left foot to rest on the heel. However, this last makes it harder to turn on to the left side. Perhaps the former method, with the right foot in the air, is nearer the basic conception of the throw. In either case the hips should be raised, and remain raised at the end, to show the throwing action. For similar reasons it looks well for Tori's arms to remain extended at the end, and for him to be looking at Uke.

Uke should remain *down* at the end of the throw; he is not now directed to rise from the Ukemi movement.

### Fine Points

This is now the only one of the Nagenokata in which two distinct attacks are made. (Formerly Tsurikomigoshi was a second example.) In many of the kata there is what is technically called 'go-no-sen' or taking the lead away from the opponent – that is to say, Uke makes an attack but Tori gains the lead and throws him. But Yokoguruma is the only case in which the lead is regained after losing it. Such waza require a high degree of skill, to adjust to a correct counter-move and launch a new attack. In Randori, Yokoguruma is traditionally connected with opponent's Koshiwaza attacks; according to Mr. Nagaoka (10th Dan) this Judo waza has not been sufficiently exploited.

In the Kata it is important that Uke should not adopt from the beginning a posture

*Left Seoi flicker (No. 6)*

Tori here adopts the sleeve hold in the final stages, a permissible variation which can get full impetus into the throw.

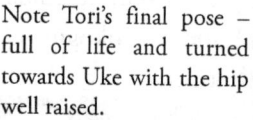

Note Tori's final pose – full of life and turned towards Uke with the hip well raised.

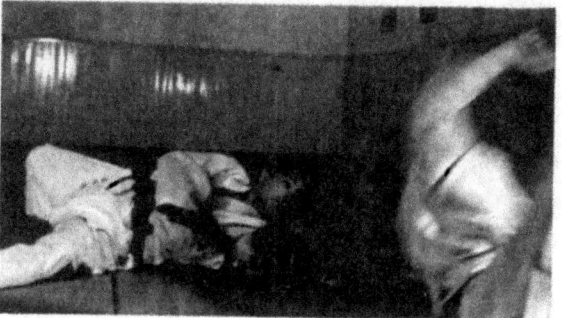

64

*Ukiotoshi flicker (No. 5)*

different from the Uranage attack; he must not show that the transition to Yokoguruma is already expected by him. This means he must be careful, when he launches his blow, not to bend forward in anticipation of the bend he will have to make after Tori comes in. This is one detail of the whole problem of keeping the Kata 'alive'; namely that Uke must never show that he knows he is going to be thrown, and is resigned or positively helping in it.

Similarly Tori must demonstrate a convincing entry for Uranage; he must not show he expects it to fail.

*Left Seoi flicker (No. 5)*

## 3. Uki-waza (Floating Technique)

Tori and Uke approach to about 3 feet apart.

| *Uke* | *Tori* |
|---|---|
| 1. Uke steps forward and adopts right 'locked' Jigotai (as in Sumigaeshi). | Tori also adopts right locked Jigotai as in Sumigaeshi. Tori floats Uke up with his right hand and pulls his right foot back in a big step. |
| Uke yields and advances his left foot. | 2. As Uke tends to adjust position (i.e. return to right Jigotai) Tori floats him up still more with both hands. |
| To preserve balance, Uke steps diagonally to his right front. . . | 3. . . . at this moment Tori uses both hands to unbalance Uke to his right front corner, lightly extends his left leg and throws himself on to his left side, taking his leg in a curve to the left back corner. Uke is thrown beyond Tori's left shoulder. |
| Uke gets up with Joseki on his left. | Tori gets up with Joseki on his right. |

Uke approaches Tori and they perform Ukiwaza from left Jigotai. Then they return to their original positions, and turn to face each other in Shizenhontai. They take one step back (right foot, left foot) so that they are now about 18 feet, (three mat-lengths) apart, and perform the Zarei or kneeling bow. They stand, face Joseki and perform the standing bow together, and then retire.

**Ukiwaza** (*Notes*)

This throw also is a difficult one, though not so tricky as Yokogake and Yokoguruma.

In the drawing Tori and Uke are just coming together for the 'locked' Jigotai; the heads have not yet settled and the left palm is about to be set on the opponent's arm.

The first step back is as in Sumigaeshi. As for the second step, Uke now gets in a full step with the right foot and Tori begins the throw as Uke is in mid-step. Tori now takes his leg well back; some authorities used to place it across in front of Uke's right foot. (The leg can in fact go much farther back than in the drawing.)

It is permissible for Tori (both here and in Sumigaeshi, as shown in the drawing) to hold Uke's outer sleeve in order to release Uke's arm a little for the Ukemi turn. This is a great help to an inexperienced Uke.

The bodies must move as one; Tori's hands can be considered as hooks. Tori's body action must synchronize with Uke's original movement, otherwise there is an unsightly jerk.

*Fine Points*

The principle is similar to Ukiotoshi. Uke manages a step with the right foot to meet Tori's pull, but Tori finds a method of unexpectedly prolonging the pull in such a way that Uke cannot adjust to meet it. Tori's left leg does not block Uke's leg from advancing, nor is there any idea of a trip. Tori swings his left leg away in order to get the full body pull.

Tori's drawing action is continuous from the withdrawal of his left foot. Care must be taken not to have the throwing action in two 'stages'. If the timing is right, Uke leaves the ground and is thrown in a very big arc through the air. Remember however that Uke stays down at the end of the throw. The final pose of all – after the second Ukiwaza – can be a tiny bit prolonged to indicate the end of the Kata.

*Left Seoi flicker (No. 4)*

# COMMENTARY

What follows is in no sense official: it is based on study on lines suggested by certain teachers expert in Kata. This kind of study has made the Kata to me much more interesting, and I pass it on in the hope that other students will find it a stimulus to their own thinking and practice.

Dr. Kano devised the Nagenokata with three aims: (1) to deepen and perfect the study of technique, and (2) as a method of physical development and education, and (3) as a means of spiritual training.

(1) His conception of technique was based on the phrase ZEN-YO, which means literally 'right use'. Right use is to include physical and psychological use, and it consists in defining the objective rightly, and then applying the most efficient means to secure it. The loose rendering 'maximum efficiency' conveys to most people only the second part, namely finding efficient means.

If we define the objective in Nagewaza, we find it is to throw an opponent, himself a skilled man, with impetus and controlled power. It is not enough merely to upset him. Sometimes Tori seems to think it sufficient just to help Uke to jump over. This is a big mistake. *In Kata the techniques must work*, and against a skilled man it is not enough merely to upset him, because he can twist or find other means of frustrating the throw. The Kata throw must be sufficiently powerful and fast to be capable of scoring a full point in a contest, and both Tori and Uke must make this clear when they demonstrate Kata.

Tori must make the throw properly. This does not mean to smash Uke down with all his force; one does not need to do that in a contest. But it does mean that his posture at the end should show that he has *thrown* Uke, and ideally that he still has power in reserve.

On his side, Uke must not rise expectantly on tiptoe before Tori even begins Tsurikomi. Nor must Uke jump over before the throw is applied.

In this light the principles guiding demonstration of the different throws will be clear. Take Ukigoshi as an example. Tori has to move quickly before Uke can adjust by relaxing his body; the whole throw depends on catching Uke while his body is stiff, and this is one reason why the throw is demonstrated as defence to a blow. Ukigoshi in Randori has to be fast, and its essence is speed, which must be shown in the Kata. Now in Haraigoshi on the contrary Uke is pinned against Tori and the throw need not be hurried; if we examine contest Haraigoshi we find the thrower takes his time over the throw, the correct action being more important – *in this case* – than speed.

(2) As to physical development and physical education, Dr. Kano devised throws in which Uke has to exert himself and display considerable skill to make his Ukemi. The Kata falls generally cover a good deal of ground and are fairly strenuous for a student. For this reason he replaced Sukuinage (in which Uke is thrown to the rear) with Kataguruma.

There is now no throw in the Kata in which Uke is thrown back, and one reason is that Dr. Kano selected what may be termed the most athletic throws from the different sections of throwing technique. Dr Kano's aim was to help Uke and Tori to build up a good all-round physique; many Judo men who concentrate in contest on only one or two techniques develop very onesidedly unless they practise Kata.

For the same reasons the throws have to be performed to right and left. (As explained in the text, the present system of classifying is rather confusing. The point is not of too much importance; it suffices here to note that Ukigoshi, Okuriashi, Sasaetsurikomi, Uranage, Yokogake, Yokoguruma, and Ukiwaza are now all done with what is termed the 'left' version first. This makes no difference to accepted practice, but is purely a question of naming.)

(3) As to spiritual training, Dr. Kano believed that by practice a man could be perfectly calm inwardly while perfectly alert and responsive outwardly, and this is one aspect of Kata training.

For those who are interested, the Budo tradition is that the expert breathes very slowly and with long breaths. 'The true man breathes from his heels, the shallow man gasps from his throat.' It was believed that thought tends to waver at the end of expiration, and following this line, some Kata experts used to begin the technique by taking in an abdominal breath, then hold it and slightly tense the abdominal muscles, and retain that condition during the execution of the waza. 'The whole body soft and the abdomen hard', is one of the sayings of this school. It was also said that a real Samurai must be able to cross the Gojo bridge in Kyoto in a single breath. (Gojo bridge was 73 yards long.) Applied to Nagenokata, this style of practice would imply taking in a deep breath as Tori and Uke approach, and holding it with a slight abdominal tension until after Uke's fall. I am not recommending this practice for Western students in general, but those interested in relation of mind and body may find it interesting.

*Tsugiashi.*

Ukiotoshi begins in Shizentai with what we may call the 'standard two steps'. (Note, however, that as explained later, these are never again made in quite the same fashion; Tori either alters the pull or else as in Sasae does not complete the second step.) Tsugiashi is used because if Uke steps in Tsuzukiashi, where the feet lead alternately, various other opportunities would arise each time the feet passed, and this would confuse the issue. Only in Tomoe will this rule be broken, and then for special reasons.

However, in Jigotai, Tsugiashi is not necessary, as the feet do not closely approach each other when passing to take the lead.

In the following commentary, the throw is taken as a unit. Thus when it is said 'this happens only once in the Kata' it means that it happens only in the particular throw. The throw is, of course, performed twice – on left and right – but this is for the sake of symmetrical development and does not affect the theory of sequence of throws.

# THE THROWS AND
# THEIR SEQUENCE

1. *Ukiotoshi.* Uke advances to take right Shizentai, and comes forward freely in response to Tori's pulls, until at the third step he is caught out by Tori's unexpectedly large third step. Tori defeats all reasonable expectations by going down on to one knee and so getting more weight into the pull besides making it longer.

According to the theory which I am now setting out (and which is not official), *Uke never again comes forward naively in this way* in the other throws. In the remaining throws which begin with what may be called the 'standard two steps' (namely Kataguruma, Haraigoshi, Tsurikomigoshi, Sasae, Yoko-gake) Tori changes his method of pull or his steps, and Uke does not lay himself open again to any of the earlier throws. If we like, we can think of Uke as learning by experience during the Kata.

Ukiotoshi is the simplest of throws in principle – rhythm is imposed on Uke, and then the very long step breaks the rhythm and Uke cannot recover psychologically in time to adapt. In Ukiwaza at the end, Tori reverts to the same principle, including the long step. Uke there is in Jigotai, which would normally be protection enough against a long pull from the upright position – but Tori finds a way of making the pull effective by throwing his whole weight into it. He extends the principle of Ukiotoshi by taking a step which is no step, because it does not keep him upright.

2. *Seoinage.* This is the first of the throws where Uke initiates the movement with *force,* as distinct from the standard two steps for instance, where he merely takes hold and then Tori initiates the movement. This first blow is straight forward and down, and Uke

75

throws himself into it without any holding back. This is an unskilled and incautious blow. Uke is made to miss completely and is thrown over. Again (according to this theory of the sequence), *Uke never again makes such a completely unchecked movement of force* (except, of course, in the left-hand version of the same throw). In the other waza which begin with a blow (Ukigoshi, Uranage, Yokoguruma), Uke is holding himself back to some extent.

3. *Kataguruma.* This begins with the standard two steps, but Uke is holding himself a trifle back and with his right leg a trifle bent and braced. Ukiotoshi would now be impossible. Tori changes his grip to throw Uke's reactions out (and also to protect his own neck), and directly attacks the mainstay of Uke's preparedness, namely the right leg.

In this throw Tori demonstrates that a man can lift much more than his own weight, by standing upright with Uke on his shoulders before throwing him. (See pictures below.)

T. Kawamura (7th Dan) showing Kataguruma

4. *Ukigoshi.* Uke again begins the movement with force, but this time does not come forward with his weight wholly on the right foot, but keeps some back on the left. In order to show this clearly, some old teachers made this blow more of a swing to the left top of Tori's head. This is now incorrect – the blow must be down. But it is clear that it is not quite the same blow as in Seoinage, because Uke's weight is on the toes of both his feet instead of entirely on the right foot.

Uke's body is quite rigid from the blow. Tori must be very fast in order to get the throw in before Uke can soften his body.

In this connection consider Ukigoshi in Randori. It only comes in as a counter to opponent's hip throw, when you can slide or jump round. Momentarily the opponent's body is rigid from the force he has put into the throw, and you have a chance for Ukigoshi, which in these circumstances is an extremely useful counter. But the throw must be very fast before opponent can soften his body and twist off the throw. This is an example of the application of Kata theory to practice.

5. *Haraigoshi.* On the second of the standard two steps, Tori puts his arm through to threaten an Ukigoshi. Uke is all set to move round this, but Tori unexpectedly blocks the leg with Haraigoshi. The historical development was explained in the section on Haraigoshi; it is an important demonstration of the need for devising newer techniques all the time. Techniques which are *mechanically* perfectly effective will, nevertheless, fail if the opponent is expecting them, in other words if they are *strategically* ineffective.

Lest anyone object that surely all the available techniques have already been found, I can say that after over thirty years' study and experience, with some of the best masters in the world, I still see techniques quite new to me. Moreover, as in Chess, old lines which are no longer studied can be revived with great success; the opponent knows that this old method is supposed to be unsound, but he has forgotten (or never knew) how to refute it.

6. *Tsurikomigoshi.* Again the standard two steps, but Uke comes out prepared to brace back against Haraigoshi. Tori has modified his grip, and is holding at the back of the neck. This anticipates Uke's movement of the left foot which he will use to help him brace back. Tori will hoist him higher than expected, and moreover this time comes in with the hips much lower than the point of application in Haraigoshi. It is these factors of the *unexpected* which throw Uke.

We can learn from Kata the importance of changing the factors. If I always hold with the same grip it is quite easy for an experienced opponent to

*Left Seoi flicker (No.2)*

learn all the distances, and all the forces which I can apply. When he has the feel of the throws he can get set, as it were, and will be very difficult to dislodge. This can be broken up by changing the points of application. Remember that, as one teacher told me, you are trying to outwit not the opponent's brain, but his bodily reactions. In contest he has no time to think, but relies on the reactions of the body as trained in Judo. 'And the body [added the teacher] is quite a stupid thing!' Even a small change will be sufficient to make a formerly successful defence reaction quite ineffective. Only real masters of Judo make fresh creative reactions each time; it is very difficult to trap them in their own reactions. But that is a peak of attainment beyond analysis.

7. *Okuriashiharai.* As soon as he engages, Tori takes Uke's breath away and imposes an unfamiliar rhythm on him. The physical body instinctively falls into any rhythm that is around – if a drum beats 'one, two, three . . .' we find we have tensed ourselves for the fourth beat. This is an important principle of Judo, and can easily be tested by experiment.

The essence of the throw is that Tori initiates the side step as soon as he takes hold; his rapid movement is meant to surprise Uke, and must surprise the audience.

Tori must not fumble or hesitate or pause, but go straight into the steps and then the throw. Uke must not jump; if his steps are correct Tori will be able to sweep him over.

There is a connection between this throw and Uchimata, where also Tori will take away the opponent's capacity for initiative by imposing an unfamiliar movement.

8. *Sasaetsurikomiashi.* This begins with the standard two steps but now Tori gets the lead by making an unusual second step. He *breaks the rhythm* of the steps by continuing his right foot past the left one; this breaking of the expected rhythm stiffens Uke's body and Tori is able to utilize that to bring him right over. When expertly performed the throw is done fast and takes the audience slightly aback, as it is supposed to take Uke.

9. *Uchimata.* As in Okuriashi, Tori initiates an unusual movement; this time Uke instead of freely following it, drags his feet so to say. He takes wide steps, making Okuriashi out of the question. Tori, however, succeeds

in securing an Okuriashi-like result by sweeping up the leading leg from inside instead of the rear leg from outside. Note that this throw must be made as a leg throw; to make it the springing-up hip throw (which Uchimata often becomes in contest) is to falsify the Kata, which includes Uchimata under the Ashiwaza or leg techniques.

Whereas, in Okuriashi, Uke was rushed into a fast sliding movement, here the sense of his movement is defensive. The throw works because Uke fancies that his wide stance protects him from throws along the line joining the feet. This is true if he is static, but

it is not true when in movement. The point is important in the analysis of many contest methods.

Uchimata is the first illustration of the so-called 'inner' throws, which are specially designed against a wide stance. We shall meet this type of throw again in Sumigaeshi, which is against a full Jigotai.

10. *Tomoenage*. For the first time in the Kata the opponents cross the feet when they have engaged. The set of three steps has been criticized on the ground that various opportunities are afforded to both sides during these steps, and it must be admitted that the objection has force. The main point, however, is that Tori is *controlling* Uke while he walks; Uke has momentarily lost the lead and has all he can do to keep his own balance. Tori does not attempt any of the Kari (reaping) throws to Uke's rear because he is attempting to secure a definite reaction.

Uke's part is enormously important, especially from the point of view of the audience. It must be clear that he suddenly recovers balance and pushes back strongly. Tori must then seem to disappear in front of him; if well done the throw illuminates a main principle of Judo.

Uke is directed to stand up after this Tomoe throw, which tends to confuse the issue in the minds of Western audiences; however, the purpose is perhaps to demonstrate the effectiveness of Ukemi. In all the other sutemiwaza Uke should now stay down.

In Tomoe a new principle is illustrated – the principle of pushing an opponent one way in order to get him to react directly back. In Budo this is called 'making the enemy's army one's own'. In Tsurikomigoshi (and to some extent in Uchimata) the opponent reacted from an anticipated throw, and in Yokoguruma the opponent will react from an attempted throw, but Tomoe is the only one where a simple push is used to provoke a direct and forcible reaction, as distinct from a mere bracing back, or attempt at evasion. Consequently Tomoe is one of the highlights of the Kata, the others being Ukitoshi and Seoinage at the beginning, Okuriashi and Uranage in the middle, and (but only if very well done) Ukiwaza at the end.

11. *Uranage.* In the sequence of throws one can suppose that the blow in Uranage is more downward, so that Seoinage and Ukigoshi would now be very difficult. Tori shoots in much more closely against Uke than in the previous two defences to a blow, where his feet were more or less in front of Uke's feet. Here Tori's feet pass well through (especially the left one) and Uke's right leg is, in fact, between Tori's thighs. With Uke's blow more downwards, it is difficult to turn him over, and consequently Tori lowers his own centre of action by falling down as he makes the throw.

If we compare Uke's centre of gravity as he goes over with its course in Seoinage, we find that in the latter Uke passed over while Tori was standing (though with knees somewhat bent), whereas here he is passing over Tori who is *on the way down to the ground.* Here is an important application of sutemi: normally at low levels the knees are very much bent and so lose mechanical efficiency, but here the low level is attained without having to bend the knees so much, and consequently Tori can get a big thrust with knees not too much bent and therefore more mechanically efficient. (The dynamics have been worked out by Judo engineers'; but anyone can try the experiment of shouldering an outsize opponent and feeling how the knees lose power as they bend more and more.)

12. *Sumigaeshi.* This is another example of the sutemi principle illustrated in the last throw, but now in another application. Uke is in Jigotai, and his centre of gravity is so low that it is almost impossible to get sufficiently far underneath for Tomoe. Nor is Uke moving freely enough to bring off Tomoe easily. Tori therefore has to use a Tomoe-like throw but with a much smaller distance between the bodies. He solves the problem by applying the foot to the thigh instead of the abdomen.

From the point of view of mechanics, if he tried Tomoe, his knee would have to be so much bent that it would lose power, whereas by applying his leg along a diagonal (really the radius of the circle of Uke's fall) he can keep his knee straighter and more effective. Note that in the Jigotai positions, both Uke and Tori are permitted Tsuzukiashi (i.e. leading with left and right foot alternately). This is permissible because in Jigotai the feet do not come close when they pass.

The first step in Sumigaesi illustrates the main method of meeting Jigotai and defence in general.

Tori wishes to throw to Uke's right front corner, but Uke, with his advanced and braced right foot, is secure against a Tsurikomi in that direction. The trick is to pull to the *other* front corner, to get Uke to advance his left foot. Now Uke's right foot, *though it has not moved,* has become the rear foot, and he is consequently statically weak to his right front.

Altogether this is a throw for the Judo audience; to other audiences it merely looks like a feebler version of Tomoe, and most of them cannot see the difference.

13. *Yokogake.* Yokogake is another throw which is difficult to execute con-vincingly. Either the sweep hits a block so to say, and Uke has to be despera-tely tugged down by Tori from the ground, or else Uke quietly removes his weight from the attacked right foot and allows Tori to sweep it away, himself standing on the left foot. Then he gently subsides in his own time.

The idea of the throw is that Tori applies a slight twist to Uke's body during the standard two steps, and this twist stretches Uke out. (The method is an important one in many variations of Ashiwaza.) Tori finishes off the throw with a sutemi method which we have not yet seen, namely, throwing the whole weight of the body into a thrust. This is what fencing masters understand by 'sutemi', and it has a psychological significance also, of keeping nothing back in reserve but hurling everything in. The key to the throw is that Tori's hips should come to the ground somewhere near the spot where Uke's right foot was standing.

An unseasoned Uke cannot be expected to take the fall in all its force; in practice he can keep some of his weight on the left foot and let Tori practise throwing himself in. Gradually Uke can allow more and more weight to come on to the edge of his right foot. In the final version, both his legs should shoot into the air as in Okuriashi.

It takes a certain amount of courage before Uke can screw himself up to the first attempt at the full fall. This is part of his training, and in a way it can be considered as a training in 'sutemi' from his side. As a consolation to the present-day Judoka, I can say that the fall in its present form is still not nearly so difficult as in some older versions where Tori was nearly in front of Uke. This throw and fall are the severest test for both Tori and Uke and it is technically the peak of the Nagenokata.

14. *Yokoguruma*. This is the representative of a small group of throws in which Uke is thrown in a very tight circle.

If we consider Seoi and Haraigoshi, we find that Uke is rotated about his centre of gravity, which is only slightly lifted if at all. In Kataguruma, Uke's whole centre of gravity is well lifted as he is rotated, and his feet describe a very wide curve. In Tomoenage, Uke is rotated about his centre while it is moving forward; in Sumigaeshi while it is moving forward and down. Now in this Yokoguruma, Uke rotates about his centre while it is moving much more sharply down. Uke has very little forward movement — he has prevented the Uranage by bending almost at right angles to the line of his blow. Tori uses what little mobility remains in the position by getting through underneath Uke and turning him over as he comes down on to Tori.

The throw is akin to the Newaza 'turnovers' in which also Uke is rotated in a small tight circle. In fact, it is extremely diffcult to secure anything like a clean point with this throw in practice; it is almost impossible to turn Uke over in the time and space available before he can straighten out. Even Mr. Nagaoka, supreme technician of Yokosutemi, frequently could do no more than bring his opponents down on their shoulder-point and then continue with Newaza.

15. *Ukiwaza*. In this throw we return to the principle of the unexpectedly long step with which the Kata began, but this time performed against Jigotai. The same method is used to overcome the static Jigotai posture as in Sumigaeshi.

There are even now several versions of Ukiwaza, depending on whether Tori lays more or less emphasis on the 'Uki' or 'floating up' of the title. I believe, however, that as an ending to the Kata it is most effective when performed on the lines of Ukiotoshi. That is to say, whereas in Ukiotoshi Tori secured an exceptionally long step by going down on to one knee, here he gets an even bigger one by giving up the normal requirement of a step, that it supports the body. He throws his body to the ground while taking his left leg back.

In this throw Uke is thrown from the shoulders (not the hips as in Uranage), and if it is well done Uke can be made to take off and shoot far clear of Tori's body. 'Throwing the hammer' gives a hint of the method. This is one of the few throws in the Rata in which Uke is thrown far away through the air, and it makes a splendid ending to the Kata, which in the last group often tends to drag.

THE DEMONSTRATION OF HOLDS

# INTRODUCTION

'Katame' is a Japanese root meaning to harden or tighten or hold still; to clench the fist, for instance, could be rendered in Japanese by this word. The Katame-no-kata, or form of Katame, is in Judo often referred to as the 'groundwork' Kata, but the last one, for instance, begins in a standing position. The Katame-waza or Katame techniques are really the methods of immobilizing the opponent, whether by restricting his movement by a technical hold, or by threat of causing pain or unconsciousness.

It is true that in general it is easier and more appropriate to use the Katame techniques at present permitted in Judo when on the ground. In this connection it may be noted that this same final technique of the Kata, namely Ashi-garami, involves a lock on the knee which would not now be permitted in contest.

The great difficulty with Katame-no-kata is to prevent its becoming 'dead' in performance. Uke has to lie still while Tori is taking up his position, and that means that a feeling of unreality begins to pervade the whole thing. This must be prevented at all costs, and while the main responsibility lies on Tori, Uke also has an important part to play.

When you take the part of Tori, you must carefully distinguish the preliminary movements from the execution of the technique. You must make it clear from your movement which is which. Tori comes into position slowly; he makes his preparations carefully, by moving Uke's arm, for instance, and keeping well balanced the whole time. It must be clear to the audience that this moving into the key position is a quite artificial thing, whose purpose is to show the audience just what is taking place. The audience must be able to see just where the hands come and how the various holds are taken.

When you are ready, you begin the execution of the waza in the same spirit as if it were a real contest. It means in effect that Tori gives a little pounce, and this shows clearly that the hold is now on and Uke is free to try its effectiveness. In the first section (Osaekomi or holds) Tori can help by giving a little Kiai shout, simultaneously abruptly tightening the hold. Uke then makes definite attempts to escape, as given in the text; he should not merely make feeble flapping movements without any spirit.

The escaping attempts by Uke have been definitely specified in the new standardized Kata which is now the definitive form recommended by the all-Japan Judo Association and the Kodokan. Uke should make them all one after another during his attempts, and he should make them look real.

In the first section, Tori puts on the hold in the proper way. When practising Katame-no-kata, Tori should try to get the hold right, light but firm. Then Uke should make real attempts to get out, to try to see whether he can break the hold. In this way Tori can check whether his own position and control are good.

In the Shime-waza (neck-lock) section and the Kansetsu (joint-lock) section, Tori must distinguish between the major movement of holding opponent, and the final minor movement of actually applying the lock. In general we can say that Tori must be in a position to hold the opponent firmly without applying the lock. In theory, unless Tori controls Uke's movement, he will not be able to get a lock on reliably; so that in practice Tori should sometimes get Uke to struggle to free himself, and see whether he can in fact hold Uke in position, without using the pressure on the neck or the pain on the joint. To make this Kata look good, Tori must show control with his whole body.

On Uke's side, he must show that his whole body is being used in most of the attempts to escape. As in Nage-no-kata, Uke must guard against giving the impression that he knows from the beginning he is going to lose; Uke must try to give the impression of life and energy. If Uke does this well, the holds and locks look much more impressive to the audience; it becomes clear that they will in fact control even a determined and skilful resistance.

The *Mairi* signal of defeat should be loud and clear, and the moment it is given both sides stop moving. This is also an important point from the point of view of demonstration effectiveness. During the preparatory movements Tori moves very slowly and Uke is generally motionless; then during the execution of the waza both sides must be full of 'kiai' or spirit, which must appear from their posture and movements; when the *Mairi* signal is given they instantly freeze, and then Tori slowly moves out of the hold. If this alternation of slow formal movement and energetic struggle is well done, the audience's attention can be captured and firmly held throughout the Kata.

Normally, after the *Mairi* signal, all Tori has to do is to move quietly out. Very occasionally, it is found that during Uke's struggles they have moved substantially across the mat. When this happens they are supposed to move back, still keeping in position, so that they end up in the original place on the mats. The only time when this point has to be practised is in the last of the Shime-waza section, when Uke rolls with Tori. Tori frequently rolls right over on to his back, bringing Uke on top of him and applying the lock from underneath. After Uke gives the *Mairi* signal, Tori must release the pressure of the lock but keep his hands in position; still holding Uke with his hands and feet, he rolls with him back to the original position with Tori on top. This movement needs a good deal of practice before it can be done neatly.

Both sides should memorize carefully the place on the mat from which they begin each section, and be careful to return to exactly the same place at the end of the section.

In this Kata, the connecting movements are enormously important to the look of the thing, and should be practised as much as the individual techniques. Nothing looks worse than hesitation and mistakes in distance and timing.

Tori must give special attention to mastering the method of moving backward and forward in the Kyoshi position, which is the key to the smooth performance of his role. Uke, for his part, must practise the method of lying down and getting up until he can perform them in a smooth unhurried movement and not as an ugly flop. Grace and balance in these apparently minor movements make a great deal of difference to the reception of the Kata by the audience.

Beginners nearly always tend to begin to rush when they get half-way through. In particular, the three Shime-waza from the rear tend to be hurried. Tori must be careful to make a distinct break between them, coming quite upright and withdrawing a couple of inches at the end of each one.

In what follows the new standard Katame-no-kata will be described together with some hints on performance, many of them taken from the classical work on this Kata by Mr. Nagaoka and Mr. Yamashita, both direct pupils of Dr. Kano, and whose book was revised by him. There will also be some descriptions of variations in the Kata, which were formerly permissible and which are now ruled out, as a guide to bringing our British Kata to a standard form. However, after studying this and other Katas for several years under Mr. Nagaoka and other masters, I may add that in practice a good deal of latitude is in fact allowed.

# OSAE-KOMI-WAZA
## (Techniques of Holding Down)

*('Standard' Text)*

Tori and Uke stand about three mat-lengths (18 feet) apart. They face Joseki, with Tori on the left and Uke on his right, and make a bow, in the standing posture.

They turn to face each other and make the sitting bow.

Both rise. They simultaneously make a step forward, first with the left foot and then with the right, coming into Shizenhontai.

Now they together take the left foot a step straight back; with the left toes up, they sink down so that the left knee comes on to the place which the left heel has just quitted. The right foot goes out to the right (thigh and calf forming roughly a right angle); the right palm is placed on the knee while the left arm hangs naturally down. This position is called *Kyoshi* (or *Kurmdori*).

Uke brings his right foot in and then advances it one step straight to the front, following up with the left (sliding along on the knee). Taking his right foot out to the right, he once more assumes the *Kyoshi* position. (*See pictures.*)

89

(*Notes*)

As explained previously, Joseki is the place of honour in the dojo or Judo hall. If there is no clearly marked place of honour, the wall opposite the door is treated as Joseki.

You must practise getting into the Kyoshi position, moving about in it, and rising from it. It is essential to be at ease in Kyoshi and able to move freely in the formal manner, as this is the basic position of the Kata. The pictures will give you the idea how to move forward. Don't forget to keep the toes of the left foot UP.

*Historical Note.* Kyoshi used to be done on the other side, i.e. left knee up, and, furthermore, Tori originally sat right back on the rear heel. This meant some of the waza came out differently; for instance, Hizagatame was done on the other side.

To move backwards you just reverse the process.

At first your knee and toes may feel awkward, but a little practice every day will give you a smooth movement. Try to keep upright and well balanced all the time.

(*Text*)

Uke puts his right hand on the mat in front of his left knee, with the fingers pointing to the left. Supporting his body on the right hand and the left foot, he raises his left knee from the ground(See photographs moving upwards on page 91). He passes his right leg through between his right hand and left foot, and extends it out to the rear past his left foot. He comes down on to his back with hips near the left heel and hands by his sides.

(*Notes*)

Uke makes the first moves of this Kata, and much of the general impression depends on whether they are skilfully performed. An expert can make these moves with smooth control and grace which fascinate even an uninitiated

audience, and make them prepared to accept later parts of the Kata which strike them as artificial. Conversely, a lurching action by Uke destroys the receptivity of the onlookers, whether Judo men or not.

The tricky moment is when the right leg is being brought through; beginners tend to collapse at the end and flop down on to their back. A clever Uke lowers himself down smoothly at almost uniform speed.

Note that the left knee remains off the ground, the foot resting on the sole. The right leg is straight out, the foot resting on the heel.

## 1. Kesa-gatame (Scarf Hold)

When Uke is on his back, Tori draws in his right foot and stands up. He comes to Uke's right side to about 4 feet away, the *Far Position,* and then goes down into Kyoshi.

Advancing with the right foot, followed always by the left knee sliding along the mats, he comes into Kyoshi about 1 foot away, the *Near Position.*

From the Near Position, Tori comes forward a little, and with both hands pulls Uke's right arm up, taking his left hand round from the outside to hold Uke's right inner sleeve. He finally clasps Uke's right arm under his own left arm.

Turning to the left, he slides the right knee under Uke's armpit. He passes his right hand under Uke's other armpit and applies it to the shoulder.

As he brings his right knee into position, he lowers the hips and applies the right side of his chest closely to the front of Uke's chest. He bends his left leg slightly at the knee and puts the inside of the leg on the mats towards the rear, while the right leg, also slightly bent, goes forward.

Tori tightens the hold by clasping his left hand fully to him.

Uke makes to free himself in different ways, for example:

He brings his left hand across to his right hand and tries an armlock on Tori's left elbow;

He tries to find a chance to get his right knee under Tori;

He tries to turn Tori over his own left shoulder. After failing in such attempts, he gives the signal *Mairi* (conceding the point) by lightly beating Tori's body, or the mats, with his hand a couple of times. (If the hand cannot be used, Uke may give the signal by beating with the foot.)

At the signal *Mairi,* Uke and Tori resume their original positions in the hold. (They must do this, after the *Mairi* signal, with all the waza.)

Tori releases the hold, and with both hands returns Uke's arm to its original position. Then he withdraws to the Near Position in Kyoshi.

(If, during the application of the hold, Uke's attempts to escape have made them travel from the original position on the mats, they return to it. The same applies with all the other waza in the Kata.)

## Kesa-gatame (*Notes*)

As Tori, you must be expert in the method of moving about in the Kyoshi position (explained previously).

You must mentally mark the places on the mat which are your Far Position and your Near Position. Most people take two of the sliding Kyoshi 'steps' to get from the Far to the Near Position.

Make the first movements of the hold, when you are moving Uke's right arm out of the way, very deliberately. Try to keep upright so that the audience can see what you are doing.

In this waza and in the next, one school made Uke initiate the movement. When Tori had come to the Near Position, as he fixed his gaze on Uke the latter made to seize Tori's left lapel with the right hand. Tori caught the arm and tucked it under his left arm, then moving smoothly into the hold. This was a very interesting sequence and absolutely in the spirit of the Kata; however, it is not now standard. But it gives a good idea of how to take up the arm in the modern method.

Practise getting into the final position smoothly. When you have got his left arm up, begin moving your knee under it. Before you have gone far with the knee, stop and rest your weight on it while you thread the right arm through. Then with your weight on the right arm and the left foot, you can keep control while your right knee finishes its movement.

Note that though this is called 'Kesa-gatame', it is not the 'Hon-kesa' hold where your right arm encircles his neck. It has now been standardized as the 'Kuzure-kesa' variation, where your right arm is under his left armpit. The position of the legs is much the same in both, but if you have been practising the Hon-kesa, you must remember that in this Kata version the position of the head is different; it is not brought forward as many teachers recommend for the Hon-kesa.

## KESAGATAME

(1) Far Position. Tori does not look hard at Uke but rather over him.

(2) Near Position. Tori is edging forward from the Near Position and is about to take up Uke's arm. It is at this point that Tori fixes his gaze on Uke, in this and many of the other waza.

(3) Taking the arm. This is the standard method. The photos on the next page show a variation.

(4) In the hold.

You put on the hold by tightening with the arms; at the same time you tighten the abdominal muscles, and some teachers say that this should produce a grunt, 'uh!' Such a small kiai can be useful in signalling that the hold is on.

Uke now makes definite and well-executed efforts to escape; he must not simply flap about in a defeatist way. Uke should normally try the three escapes recommended, once each in the order given, and with sufficient energy for Tori's counter-measures to be clearly effective.

86

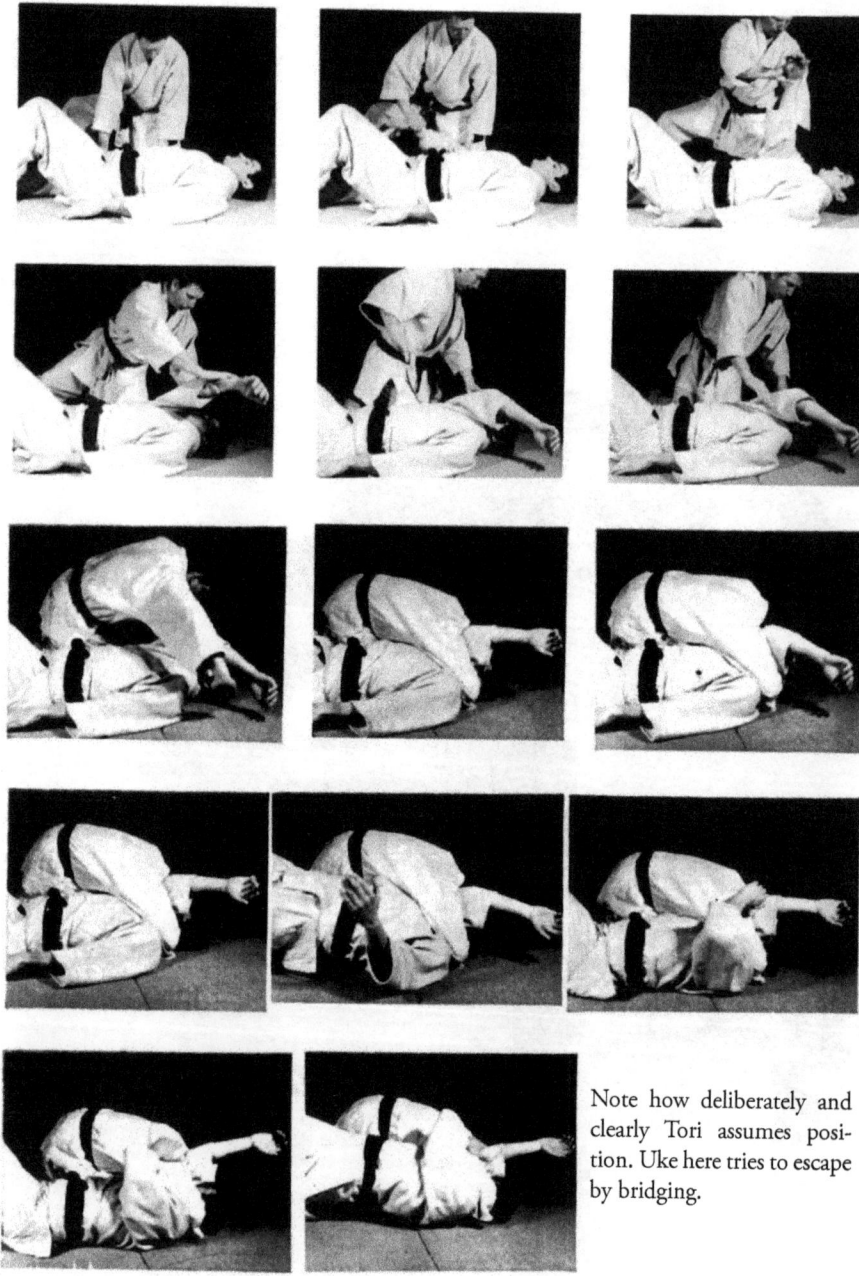

Note how deliberately and clearly Tori assumes position. Uke here tries to escape by bridging.

## KATA-GATAME (Shoulder Hold)

(1) Lifting the arm.

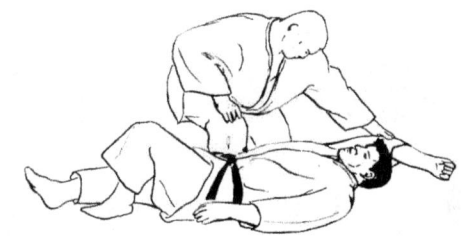

(2) Placing the arm to
side of Uke's head.

(3) The hold – taken from the opposite side to show leg position.

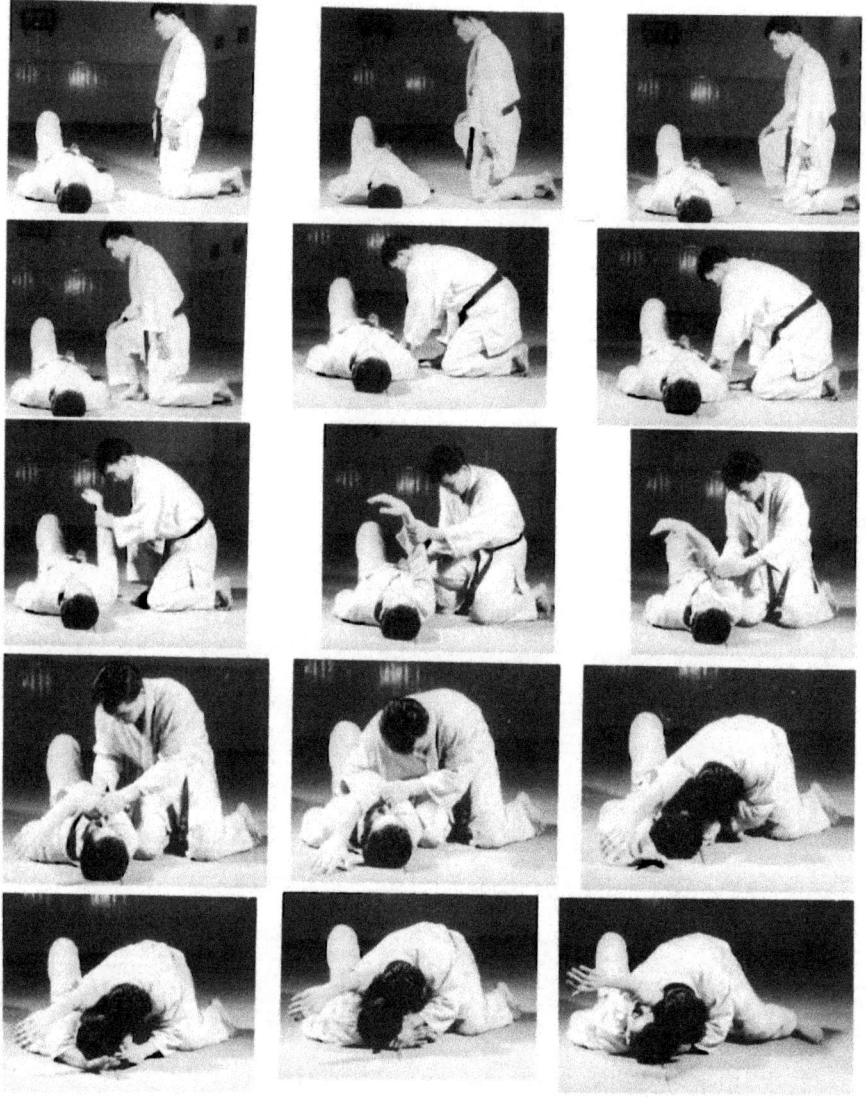

Kata-gatame from the side, to show the foot position clearly. Tori here grips his right wrist with the left hand, which is a common variation.
Note the position of the left leg in the final stages.

## 2. Kata-gatame (Shoulder Hold)

Tori comes forward slightly from the Near Position and with both hands takes up Uke's right arm. (His left hand, fingers uppermost, goes on to the upper arm, and the right hand, fingers down, holds Uke's wrist.)

With his left hand he pushes Uke's elbow against the right ear, while he brings his right knee, with the toes of the foot upright on the mat, against Uke's side.

Tori's right hand goes over Uke's shoulder and under his neck, to come out on Uke's right. Tori now applies the right side of his neck to the place which he has been pushing with his left hand. Thus pressing Uke's right arm against his cheek, he clasps his hands, with the right one on top.

Tori stretches his left leg to the side to get a purchase.

Tori puts on the hold by tightening his hands.

Uke makes attempts to free himself, for example:

Cupping his left palm round his right fist, he tries to loosen the hold by straightening the elbows;

By twisting his body to the right, he tries to get his right knee under Tori's hip;

He attempts a backward somersault over his left shoulder.

Failing to escape, he gives the signal *Mairi.*

Tori releases the hold and with both hands returns Uke's right arm to its original position.

He goes back to the Near Position (in Kyoshi) and then withdraws to the Far Position.

**Kata-gatame** (*Notes*)

This is a fairly easy one.

When you clasp the hands, hold the right hand with the fingers together and the thumb separated, and the palm down. Then bring the left hand, fingers together and palm upwards, and fit the thumb in between the right thumb and forefinger. The hands are then firmly locked together at right angles.

Uke needs to practise the back somersault to make it look convincing. He can help by pushing his own hips with his left hand.

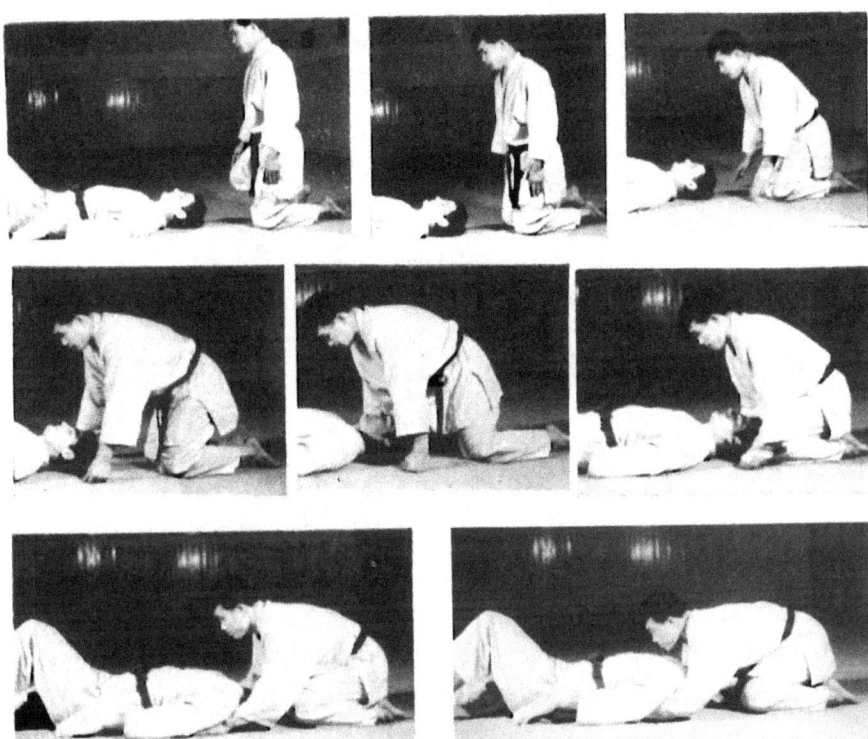

Tori coming down from Kyoshi and going into the hold. Tori here has his toes flat on the ground which is now the orthodox Kata method, though in many cases at least one leg has to be extended to cope with Uke's struggles

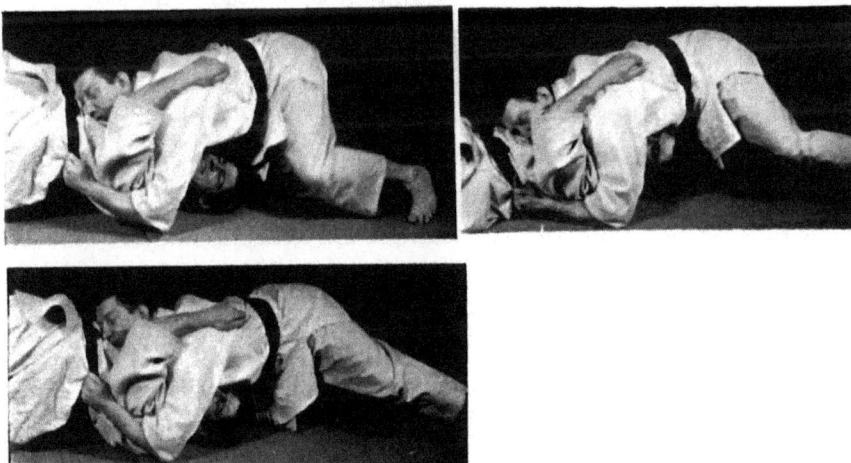

### 3. Kami-shiho-gatame (Upper Four-quarters Hold)

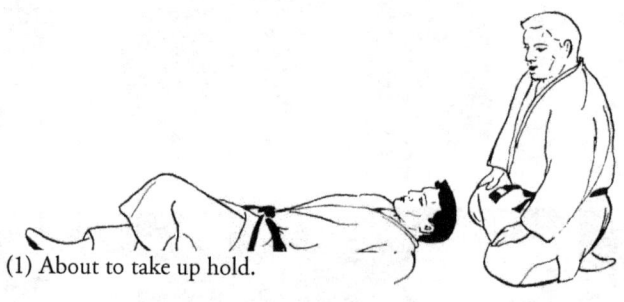

(1) About to take up hold.

(2) In position.

Tori stands up and goes round to Uke's head, there taking up the Far Position facing Uke. Advancing in Kyoshi, he comes to the Near Position.

Again coming forward a little, he puts his right knee down and thrusts both hands under Uke's shoulders, to grasp Uke's belt in the normal hold (thumbs in), thus controlling Uke's arms by his own arms.

He puts his chest on to Uke's chest and turns his head to the side.

Tori flattens his toes on to the mat, lowers his hips, and so comes into the hold.

Uke makes attempts to free himself, for example:

Trapping Tori's head with one arm and swinging (with legs and body), he tries to turn him over to the opposite side;

He thrusts an arm through Tori's armpit and twists his body;

He lifts Tori up, and by slipping back tries to get a knee or foot in.

Failing to escape, he gives the signal *Mairi*.

Tori releases the hold and returns to the Near Position in Kyoshi, and then to the Far Position.

### Kami-shiho-gatame (*Notes*)

In practice and contest this hold is now almost always put on with Tori's legs extended. Be careful you do not do this in the Kata; the knees must be well forward, and you should be as flat as possible.

Some teachers have their knees underneath them; others spread the knees. In either case the knees must, of course, be as flexed as possible. But once Uke struggles, you may extend a leg if necessary.

Again, in practice, Tori usually has his body at an angle to Uke, whereas in the Kata the two bodies are in one straight line.

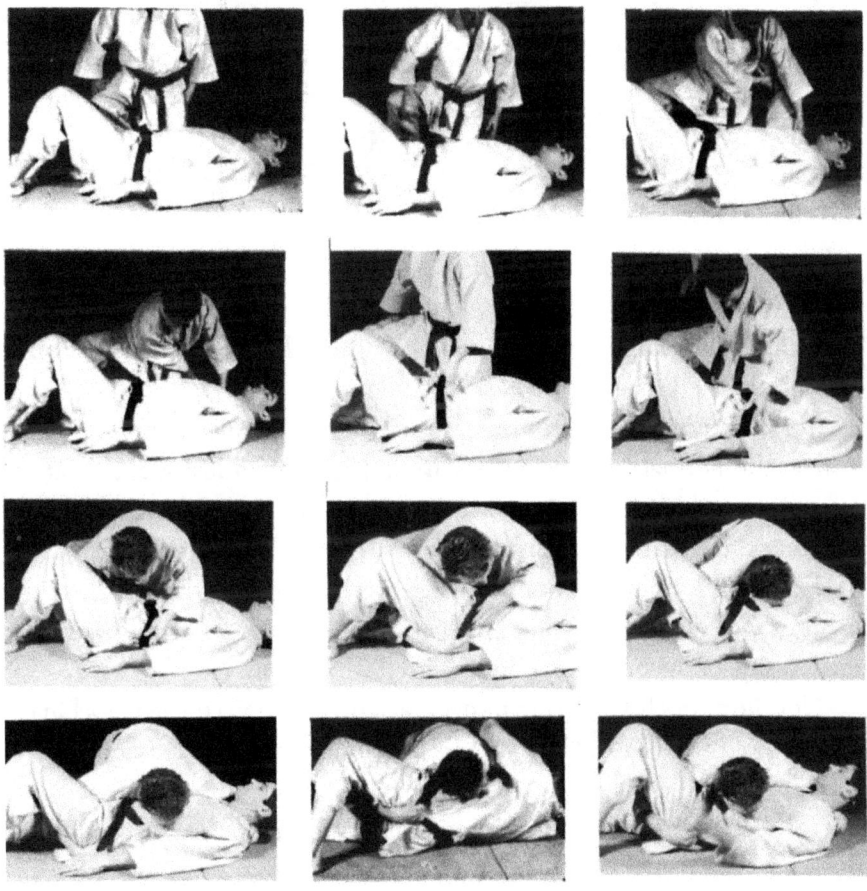

## 4. Yoko-shiho-gatame (Side Four-quarters Hold)

Tori stands up and goes to Uke's right side. He takes up the Far Position in Kyoshi, then advances to the Near Position.

Tori advances a little from the Near Position. He picks up Uke's right arm in the normal hold (palm down) and takes it to his own left, at the same time pushing his left knee against Uke's right armpit (keeping his toes upright on the mat). With his left hand he grips Uke's left-side belt.

Keeping his right toes up, he lowers his right knee, and inserts his right hand between Uke's legs, under the left thigh and past the left hip, to grasp the left side of the belt in the normal hold (thumb in).

Now he passes his left hand under Uke's neck to grasp the left lapel in the normal hold (thumb in). Tori's knees are closely against Uke's right armpit and hip.

Tori flattens his toes on to the mat, turns his head to the left, and applies the hold.

Uke makes attempts to free himself, for example: Applying his left hand to the left of Tori's neck, he tries to bring his left leg on top of it;

Twisting the hips, he tries to get his right knee under Tori's body; Gripping the side of the belt with his left hand, he tries to take Tori over with a big swing.

Failing to escape, he finally gives the signal *Mairi*.

Tori releases the hold, replaces Uke's right arm, takes up the Near Position, and then withdraws to the Far Position.

## Yoko-shiho-gatame (*Notes*)

In taking up the hold, Tori in effect first holds the belt with his left hand, and then passes it across to his right hand as it comes through the legs.

Some authorities perform this hold with the left leg stretched, and only the right knee closely against Uke. In any case, the spirit of the hold is the so-called 'control with a loose rein'; Uke has considerable freedom of movement in this hold, and so Tori has to adjust his position with great flexibility. This is an old form of the hold, not now used much in practice.

(1) Passing the belt.

(2) The hold.

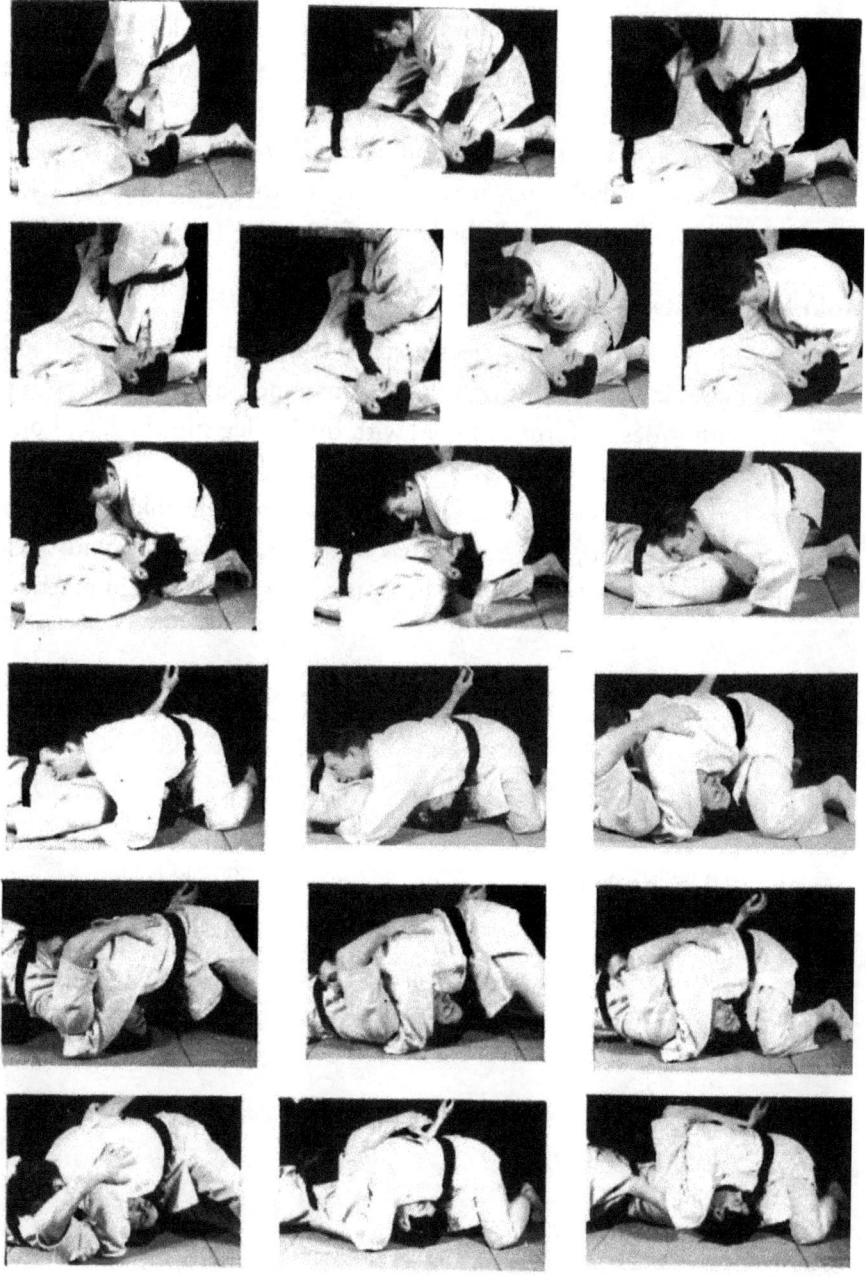

Tori lifts up Uke's head a little with his left hand to help himself to grasp the collar at the back with his right hand.

Note that Tori moves his legs and body freely to counter Uke's struggles.

## 5. Kuzure Kami-shiho-gatame (Loosened Upper Four-quarters Hold)

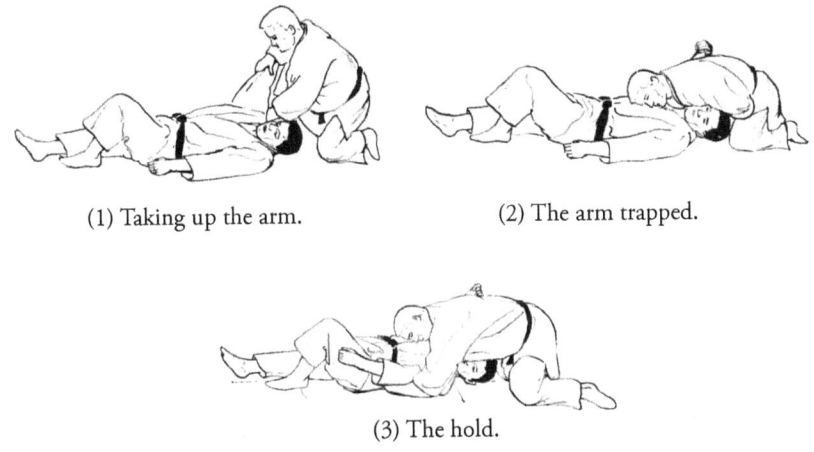

(1) Taking up the arm.                    (2) The arm trapped.

(3) The hold.

Tori stands up and goes round to Uke's head, assuming the Far Position and then the Near Position.

Tori comes straight forward a little, and then a little to his right front corner, moving the right foot first. With his right hand he picks up Uke's right arm from the inside, and with the help of his left hand, thrusts it under his right armpit.

He inserts his right hand under Uke's armpit and deeply through under the shoulder, to grasp the back of the neck in the normal hold (palm up).

He rests his right arm, thus encircling Uke's right arm from below, on his right thigh. He inserts his left hand underneath Uke's left shoulder to hold the left side belt in the normal hold (thumb in), flattens his toes, and lowers his hips.

Tori bears down with his chest rather diagonally across Uke's right chest, and applies the hold by pulling in with both hands.

Uke makes attempts to free himself, for example:

Applying his left hand to Tori's neck, and pushing with his right hand at the joint of the right thigh, he tries to slip down and back and get his right arm out for a twist to the right;

Getting his left hand through at the throat and pushing up, he tries to get his left knee in;

Gripping Tori's belt with the left hand, he tries to swing him over to the left.

Failing to escape, he finally gives the signal *Mairi*.

Tori releases the hold, and with both hands returns Uke's right arm, adopts the Near Position, and then withdraws to the Far Position.

## Kazure Kami-shiho-gatame (*Notes*)

Note that here again the hold begins with the knees bent and the toes flattened. Most Westerners find this position uncomfortable and insecure. Once Uke begins his struggles it is, of course, permissible to stretch one or both legs to counter the escape attempts. But the hold should begin in the proper way.

Some authorities used to insist on holding the neck in the reverse hold, with the fingers inside, and palm down.

## Conclusion of Osae-komi Section

Tori retreats two steps in Kyoshi, resuming the position he was in at the beginning of the Kata.

Uke meanwhile sits up, puts his right hand behind his right thigh, and supporting himself on his right hand and left foot, lifts his hips and turns to the right, bringing his right foot through. He comes on to the left knee and takes the right knee up. Thus he is now facing Tori in Kyoshi.

## (*Notes*)

Uke's movement here is the reverse of his lying down movement at the beginning of the section.

Tori and Uke should rehearse their movements so that they finish together, facing each other and looking into each other's eyes briefly.

*Section Two:*
# SHIME-WAZA
# (Neck – Lock Techniques)

Kata-juji: 'Coming In'

'Moving the Arm'

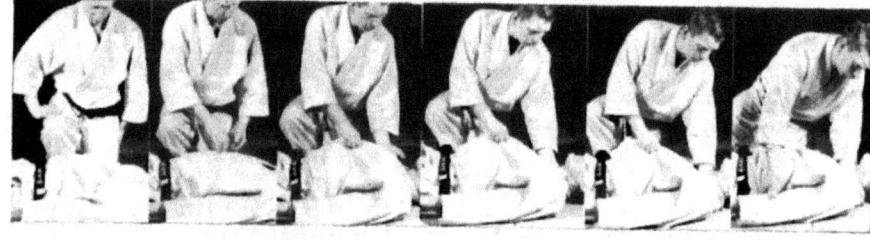

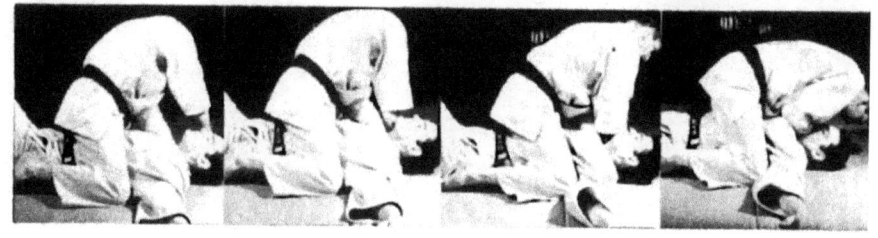

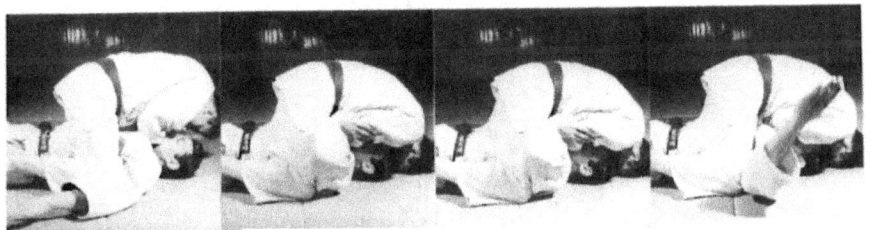

'Taking the Hold'

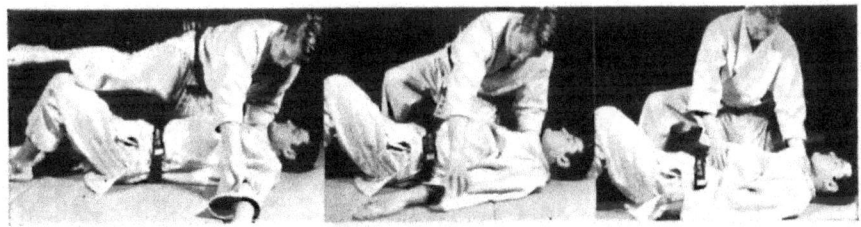

'Moving Out'

# KATAJUJI

(1) Uke's right arm has been moved out of the way: Tori inserts his left hand.

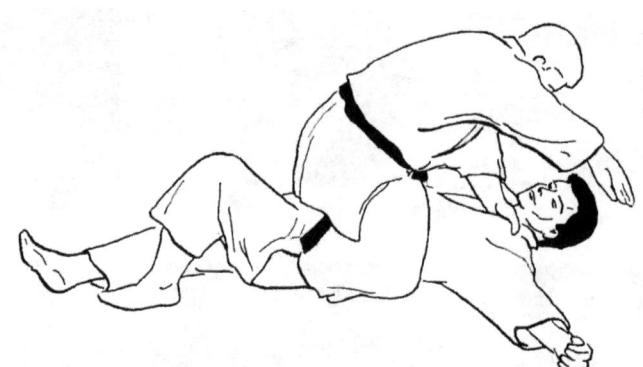

(2) Tori bringing the right hand over.

(3) The pressure on; note grip by feet.

## 1. Kata-juji-jime (Single Cross Shime)

Uke lies down on his back, as at the beginning of the previous section.

Tori rises, advances to Uke's right side, and adopts Kyoshi, facing Uke in the Far Position. Then, leading with the right foot, he comes to the Near Position.

Coming a little closer, Tori takes Uke's right arm with both his hands, moving it to his own left side. He again comes closer. His left hand grips Uke's left eri far in, in the reverse hold (fingers inside). With his right hand he pushes Uke's left arm away and then kneels astride, controlling Uke with both legs.

He takes his right hand round above Uke's head and grips the right eri in the normal hold (thumb inside). Now he makes a scissors action of the hands so that they come across Uke's throat.

Tori gives a pulling action to his left hand and a pushing action to his right, leans forward on to Uke and applies the shime pressure to his neck.

Uke seeks relief by pushing at Tori's arms with his hands; unable to escape he gives the signal *Mairi*.

Tori releases the shime.

He returns to the Near Position in Kyoshi, replacing Uke's right arm with both his hands.

Then he withdraws to the Far Position.

## Kata-juji-jime (*Notes*)

Tori should practise getting astride Uke neatly; a very small Tori can support himself on his left knee and right foot when astride, but in general both knees should be on the ground.

The manual by Nagaoka and Yamashita says that there is a tendency to put too much force into the hands and arms; instead of trying to effect the shime with the hard edges of the wrist, it is better to consider the wrists and hands as continuations of a single cord with the eri.

The right hand should hold deeper than the left.

Opponent's body is gripped with the feet, and Tori leans well forward so that his weight comes on to the hands. He should not hunch over Uke.

Tori should put his hands in with great deliberation, and take them away similarly, so that the audience have a good chance to see how the hold is taken up.

'Shime' means literally to tighten, or to wring, or to tie on a belt, and so on. The shime action is not aimed at cutting off the breath, but tightening all round the neck.

This, and all the subsequent techniques, are *holds* as well as locks. In practising them Tori should check his position by seeing whether he can maintain it against Uke's struggles, *without applying the lock.*

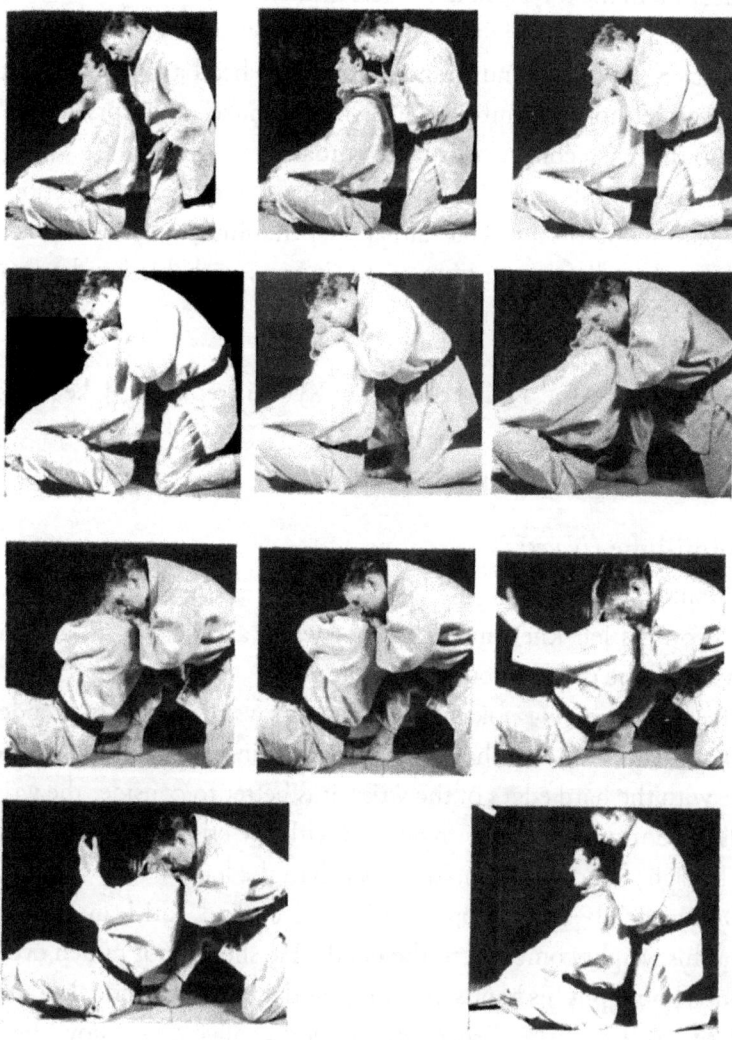

Note how Tori pulls Uke well back to unbalance him. After trying to pull Tori's right elbow down, Uke gives the *Mairi* signal by clapping his hands. Tori then sets Uke upright before slowly removing his hands and straightening up.

## 2. Hadaka-jime (Naked Shime)

Uke sits up with a straight back; he bends his left knee so that his toes come near the back of the right knee, which is slightly bent.

As Uke sits up, Tori goes round and comes into the Far Position behind Uke. Then he comes forward to the Near Position.

Tori comes forward a trifle so that he touches Uke's back. He passes his right hand over Uke's right shoulder, bends the arm so that his wrist comes against Uke's throat, and clasps his palms (the right one on top) above Uke's left shoulder. The hands interlock as in Kata-gatame (see *Notes*, p. 103).

He controls Uke by pressing his right cheek against Uke's left cheek.

Tori lowers his body by withdrawing to the rear, beginning with the left foot, and unbalances Uke to the rear.

He applies the shime to the neck by pulling in with both hands.

Uke seizes Tori's right upper arm with both hands and tries to free himself by pulling down.

Failing to escape, he gives the signal *Mairi*.

Tori releases the hold and withdraws to the Near Position.

## Hadaka-jime (*Notes*)

Tori should straighten himself up when he gets against Uke's back at the beginning. He should put the hands in with deliberation.

When he pulls Uke back, Uke should be about 45 degrees from the vertical. Tori can make this movement more quickly, but he should be careful not to make Uke choke badly.

Uke often gives the signal *Mairi* by clapping his hands in this and the two following.

Uke should make one definite attempt to pull Tori's right arm down, during which he may move his feet; he need not prolong his struggles and can give the *Mairi* signal immediately afterwards. Then he sits up straight again and replaces his feet if they have moved.

Tori *must not* press his right shoulder against the back of Uke's head, as this creates a spine lock, instead of a shime.

Again Tori should practise holding Uke in position, against Uke's best struggles, without having recourse to the lock.

(1) Taking position (from the front).

(2) Hadaka-jime on.

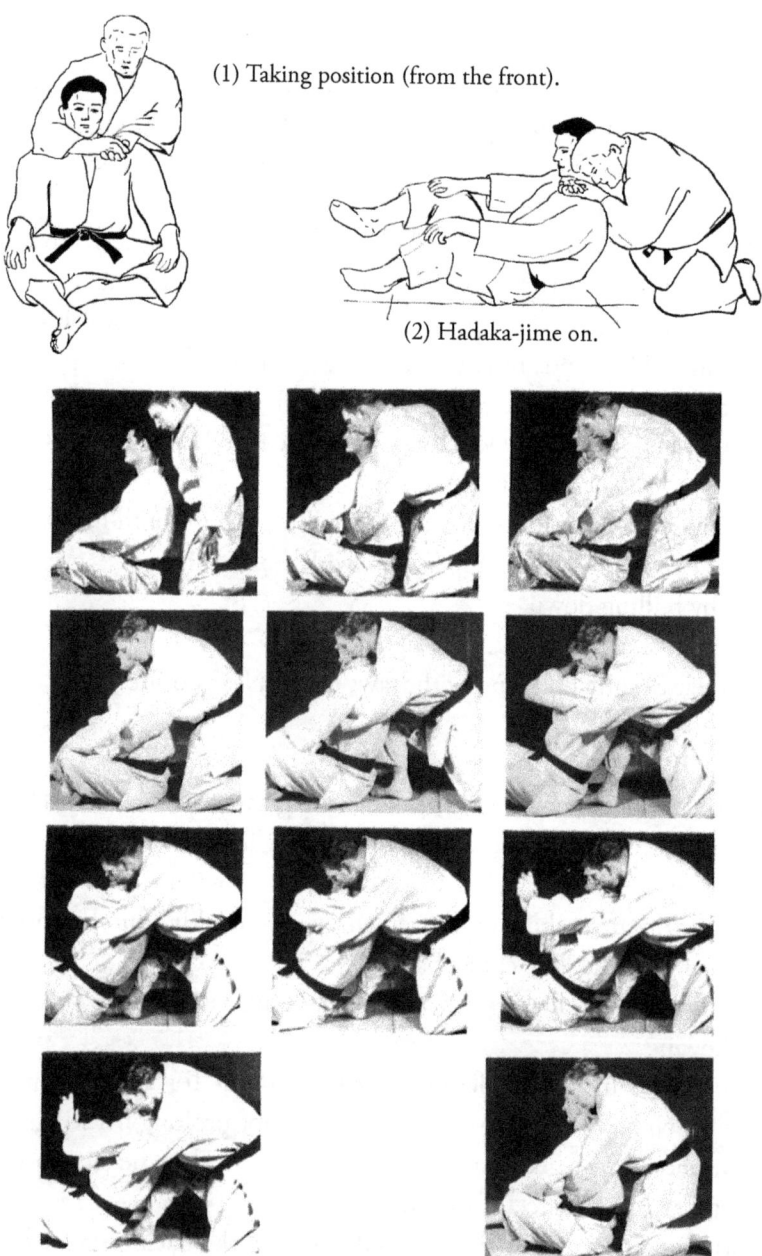

Tori breaks Uke's balance well to the rear, withdrawing his left leg.

After the *Mairi* signal, Tori sets Uke upright before removing his hands and straightening up, which he must do before going into the next technique.

## 3. Okuri-eri-jime (Sliding Eri Shime)

Tori comes forward a little from the Near Position behind Uke so that he touches Uke's back.

Tori thrusts his left hand under Uke's left armpit to grasp the left eri, which he pulls down. His right hand passes over Uke's right shoulder and comes across the throat to grip the left eri deeply in the normal hold (thumb inside).

Now he moves his left hold to a grip down on the right eri, sets his right cheek against Uke's left cheek and his right front shoulder against the back of Uke's neck. In this way he controls Uke. These moves bring Uke under complete control.

Tori lowers his body, and, moving back a little (beginning with the left foot), he breaks Uke's balance by pulling him back and down so that now Uke's weight comes lightly upon Tori's right knee.

Tori's right hand pulls in a twisting action and his left hand pulls down so that Uke's neck is constricted.

Uke seeks relief by catching at Tori's right upper arm with both hands and pulling it. Unable to escape, he gives the signal *Mairi*.

Tori releases the pressure and withdraws to the Near Position.

## Okuri-eri-jime (*Notes*)

Tori *must* have withdrawn to the Near Position (about 1 foot away) and come forward against Uke afresh. Tori often forgets and just makes these three shime from the rear in quick succession, but the Kata form is that they must be separated.

From the front.

Tori pulls Uke back to about 45 degrees.

Here again the hands and eri act, as it were, like one single cord, and the hands should not be too hard. The right hand should grip well up the eri. The left hand should hold somewhere near the level of the right hand. But some experts hold as low as in the drawing.

In one style the top of the head used to be placed against the back of Uke's neck, but now the side of the head is used as in Hadaka-jime. The shoulder comes against the back of the head, as it does *not* in Hadaka-jime. The aim is to give Uke no play for moving his head and neck.

Tori must practise keeping a good firm posture when he applies the shime; his toes should grip the ground.

Uke's escaping attempt is to pull Tori's right arm forward and up, and to slide himself forward and down out of the hold.

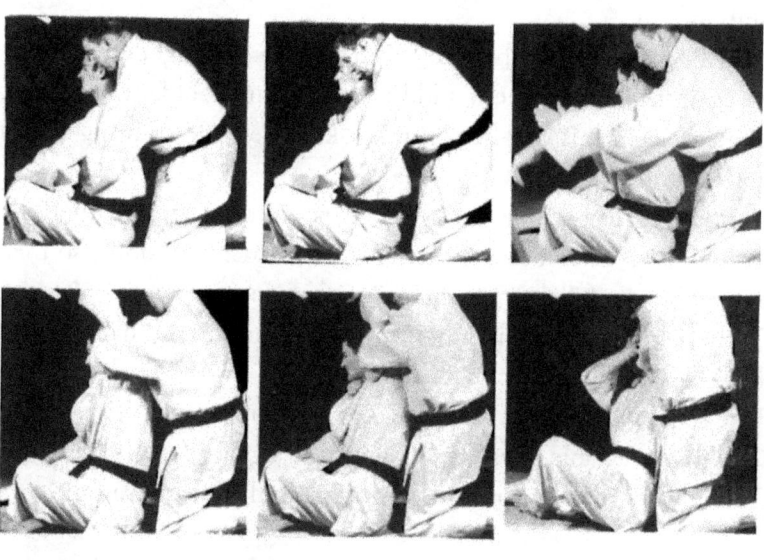

Tori breaks Uke's balance to the rear.
The action is shown from the other side
(i.e. from a point opposite Joseki) in the
last three pictures.

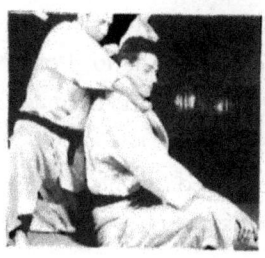  

## 4. Kata-ha-jime (One Wing Shime)

Tori, in the Near Position behind Uke, comes forward slightly to come against Uke's back.

Tori inserts his left hand under Uke's left armpit and pulls the left eri down. His right hand goes across Uke's right shoulder and past the throat, to grasp the left eri deeply in the normal hold (thumb inside).

With his left arm Tori bears against Uke's left elbow, swinging it out to the side and then right up. Thus controlling Uke, he breaks his balance to the rear. Tori's left hand, palm turned in and fingers extended, is taken over Uke's left shoulder and thrust well through under Tori's own right arm. Tori moves his right foot a trifle to the right, and, turning a little to the right, pulls with his right hand so as to constrict Uke's neck.

Uke catches Tori's left wrist with his right hand and tries to pull the left arm down. Failing to escape, he gives the signal *Mairi*.

Tori releases the pressure and withdraws first to the Near Position and then to the Far Position.

## Kata-ha-jime (*Notes*)

Tori should not grasp too shallowly or too deeply with his right hand; he must calculate it so that his right wrist, which must not be bent, is against the side of Uke's neck, and his hand across the throat when the shime comes on.

As before, think of the right hand not like a stiff pole but a continuation of the cord of the eri.

Uke in this one is unbalanced to the right rear corner; the left arm is thrust through as Uke is pulled back. The back of the wrist goes against the back of Uke's head. The left wrist and fingers should be straight. Be careful not to push Uke's head forward (though some teachers have taught this). The hand used to go sometimes above Tori's own right arm; now it always has to go below it.

Tori should watch his own posture and keep it stable.

From the front.

121

## Gyaku-juji-jime

Tori should practise holding Uke firmly between his feet during the two rolls, or else this one can become very slovenly to look at.

Uke's final struggle is generally very brief before he gives the *Mairi* signal.

From the front.

## 5. Gyaku-juji-jime (Reverse Cross Shime)

Uke lies down on his back.

When Uke is down, Tori stands up, moves to Uke's right and takes up the Far Position in Kyoshi, facing Uke. Then he advances as before to the Near Position.

From the Near Position he comes forward slightly and with both hands moves Uke's right arm round to his own left side. Again coming closer, he takes a deep hold of Uke's left eri with bis left hand, in the reverse hold (fingers in). With his right hand he pulls Uke's left arm out and away, and sits astride of Uke. Holding him between his legs, he thrusts his right hand over his own left wrist, to take a deep reverse hold on the right eri.

Pulling up with both hands, Tori leans forward over Uke and applies the pressure to his neck. Uke tries to relieve the pressure by pressing down Tori's left elbow with his right hand, and pushing at the right elbow with his left hand. Tori adapts to this by rolling to the left, with Uke between his legs, gripped by his feet.

Uke tries, as before, to relieve the pressure by pushing at the elbows, but failing to escape, gives the signal *Mairi*.

Tori releases the lock and Uke lies down on his back in the original position. Tori returns to his shime position astride Uke, then withdraws first to the Near Position and then to the Far Position.

Now Tori goes back to the original position in which the Kata began: Uke, meanwhile, sits up and resumes Kyoshi, facing Tori.

## Gyaku-juji-jime (*Notes*)

In getting astride, Tori must secure his own stability and also control opponent. If he is very small he can have one knee up; generally both are on the ground, and he grips Uke's knees with his feet when they roll.

Both hands go in about the same depth. Originally the second hand (the right) used to go in under the other, but it is now standardized to go in on top.

The shime is on the blood vessels of the neck, and also to some extent on the throat. The hands should not be rigid as if sticks, but thought of as continuation of a cord.

As in Randori, Uke's best chance is to roll towards the underneath hand, i.e. to his own right. Uke tries to push the upper elbow over his own head as he rolls.

In the old days a permissible variation was for Tori to lock his feet beyond Uke in the final position, but now he simply makes a pincer action of his knees and feet on Uke's sides and hips. It is not necessary for Tori to roll right over on to his back, though he often does so. If he does, he should hold Uke to him, after releasing the pressure, and together roll back to the original position.

*Section Three:*

# KANSETSU-WAZA
## (Lock Techniques)

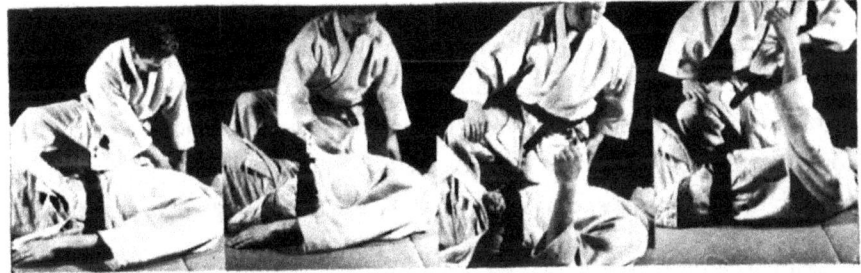

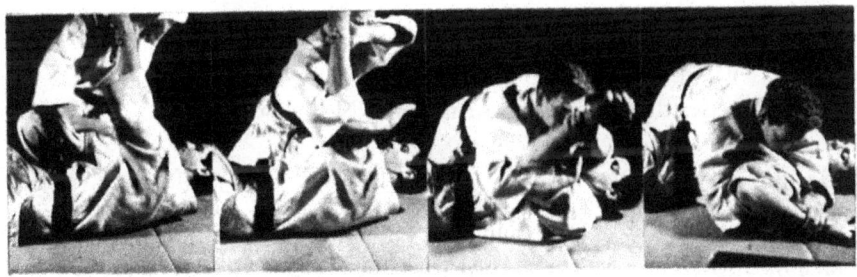

Note how the arm is laid to the side in the first six pictures. This movement, which occurs again and again, is here shown very clearly.

The final position of the arms must be carefully studied. Tori's right forearm crosses Uke's upper arm at about a right angle.

## 1. Ude-garami (Arm Winding)

When Tori has returned to his original place, both face each other in Kyoshi. Then Uke lies down on his back as before.

Tori rises and goes to Uke's right side, assumes Kyoshi in the Far Position, and then advances to the Near Position.

From the Near Position, Tori comes forward a little and with both hands picks up Uke's right arm, which he transfers to his own left side. He again comes slightly closer as if to attack Uke, who meets this by reaching up with his left hand to grasp the right eri.

Tori seizes the raised wrist with his left hand (thumb down). Putting his right knee on the mat, he presses the united left hands down to the mats somewhere above Uke's left shoulder. Uke's forearm and upper arm end up roughly at right angles. Tori's right hand now goes under Uke's arm to grip Tori's own left wrist. Bringing down his chest on to Uke's, Tori pulls with both hands, effecting a lock on Uke's elbow.

Uke turns his left wrist in and tries to escape by raising his left shoulder and hip, but failing to free himself gives the signal *Mairi*.

Tori releases the lock and returns to the Near Position.

## Ude-garami (*Notes*)

Tori waits until Uke's arm is fairly straight before catching it. Uke should make his movement definite and reasonably fast.

Tori must be holding Uke's body firmly with the knees and body.

Tori must not lift his right shoulder when putting on the lock.

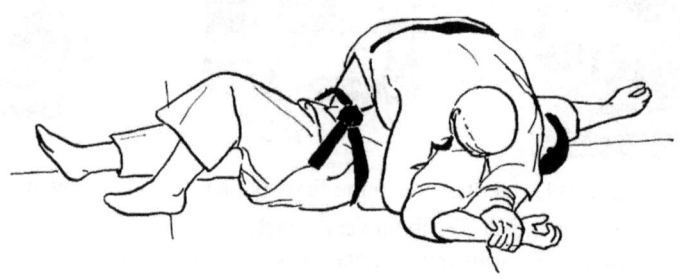

Final position,

 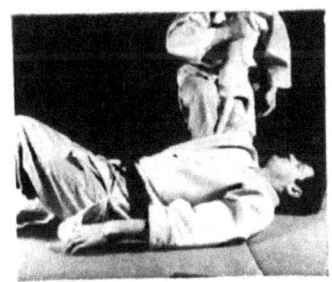

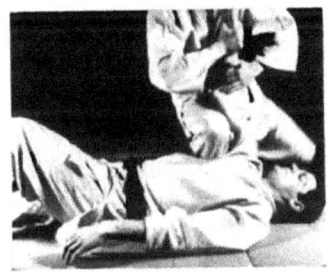 

The pincer action of the legs is most important. Tori should be able to hold Uke in the final position with his legs alone.
To come out, sit up and try to reverse the movements.

## 2. Juji-gatame (Cross Hold)

Tori comes forward slightly from the Near Position as if to make an attack.

Uke responds by stretching out his right hand to grasp Tori's left eri.

Tori grips Uke's right wrist with his right hand, aided by the left just beside it, and pulls the wrist tightly up to his chest. He pushes his right toes well under Uke's right side, bends forward and swings his left leg in an arc round over Uke's head, bringing the heel down on to the mats above Uke's left shoulder.

Tori traps Uke's upper arm between his thighs and falls back so that his body is at right angles to Uke and hips come close to his right heel. He holds Uke's neck (with his left leg) and presses his knees together. When he raises his hips a lock comes on Uke's elbow.

Uke lifts his hips and tries to free himself by pulling out his arm and twisting to the left. Failing to escape he gives the signal *Mairi*.

## Juji-gatame (*Notes*)

Here again Uke's arm should not be taken before it is fairly well extended.

Tori pulls the wrist up with both hands, and should not go down until Uke's arm is well straightened.

Tori must control Uke so that he can neither bend the arm nor twist it, nor twist his body. Tori's right foot should be well under Uke.

Moving into position.

Some teachers twist Uke's arm to the right as they make this lock, but in general the lock is applied by raising the hips and pulling the wrist a little to the right. Strictly speaking, the elbow should be pushed towards the thumb-side, and the wrist pulled towards the little finger side of Uke's hand. This brings the lock on effectively however Uke twists his arm.

Tori must remember to give Uke time to try his escape attempts before putting on the lock fully.

The full name of this technique is Ude-hishigi Juji-gatame, but it is generally called Juji-gatame for short, as there are two other Ude-hishigi ('arm crush') techniques in this Kata alone, and still others in Randori.

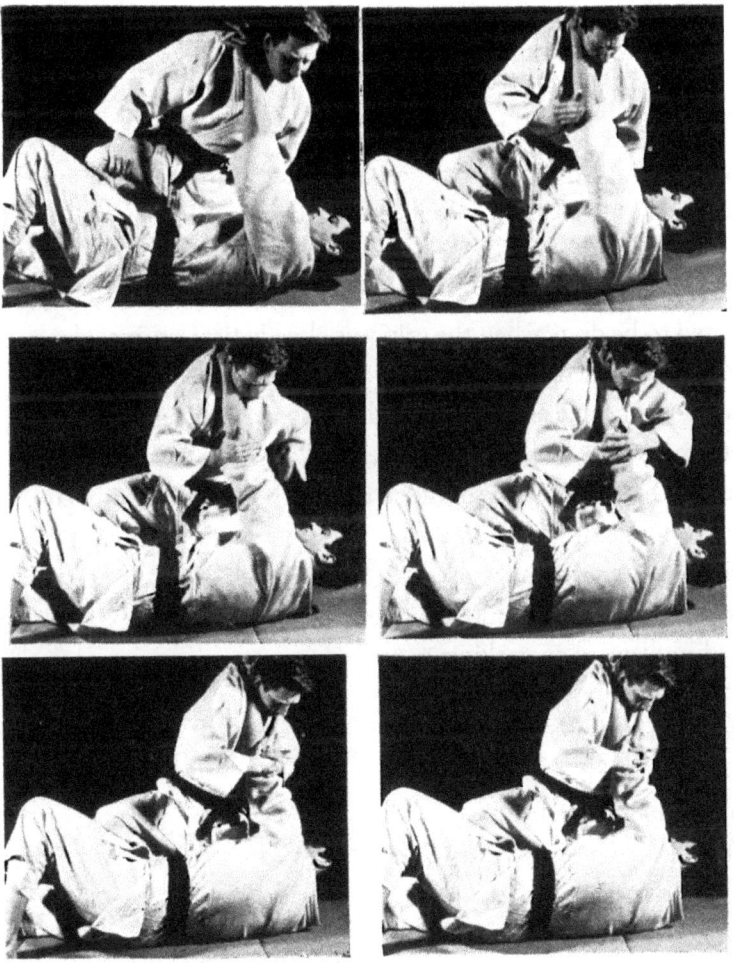

Tori must trap the arm between shoulder and neck as Uke comes to take hold. Note the slight twist as the lock is put on. Tori's right knee would usually come over Uke's body.

### 3. Ude-gatame (Arm Hold)

Tori advances slightly from the Near Position and with both hands picks up -Uke's right arm and moves it to his own left side. Then he comes a little closer as if to make an attack.

Uke responds by stretching out his left hand to grip Tori's right eri.

Tori lowers his body and catches Uke's left wrist between his right shoulder and neck. He applies his right palm to Uke's left elbow, and puts his left hand on top of it. His right shin goes against Uke's lower ribs to prevent his rising. Tori applies the lock by pulling in with both hands in a shallow curve like the keel of a ship, at the same time turning his body to the left.

Uke tries to free himself by pulling his left arm free, but failing to escape, gives the signal *Mairi*.

Tori releases the lock and with both hands replaces Uke's right arm. He withdraws to the Near Position and then to the Far Position. Tori goes round to Uke's head and Uke gets up so that they face each other in Kyoshi.

### Ude-gatame (*Notes*)

This used to be done when the grip was already firm on Tori's lapel, the arm fairly fully extended. The hands were applied rather on the shoulder side of Uke's elbow and the arm was strongly twisted to the left.

At present the lock is applied before Uke has taken hold. Uke's arm is pinned by Tori's neck and shoulder, and his body is pinned by Tori's knee.

Don't pull upwards too much or Uke's arm may slip out; there is, however, a slight upward movement in making the lock. If Tori is very much smaller than Uke, he may rise to a half standing position when putting on the lock.

The full name is Ude-hishigi Ude-gatame.

Near final position.

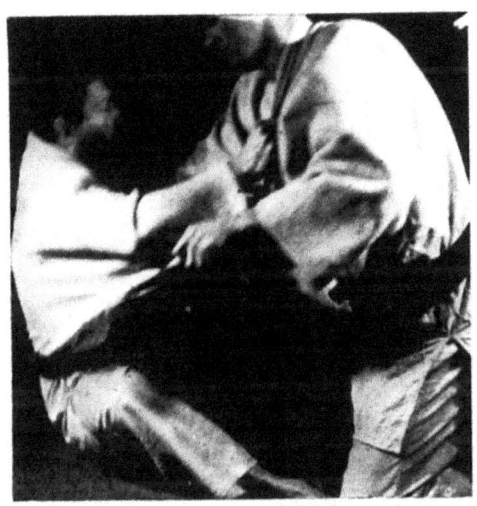

These three pictures are taken from opposite Joseki. Tori is thus on the left. From Joseki he would be on the right.

Tori secures Uke's arm (as shown in the drawing), then pushes at Uke's leg and falls back, bringing his left leg over to trap the arm. Tori's right foot is lower than usual. Compare with drawing.

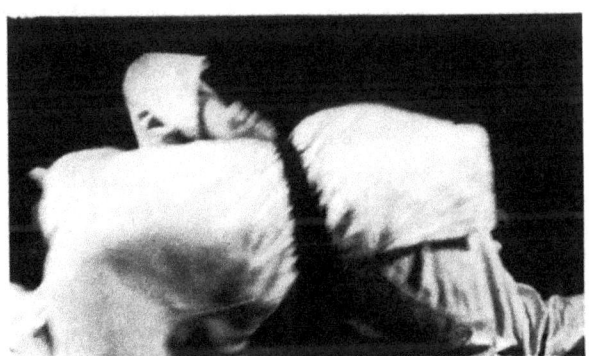

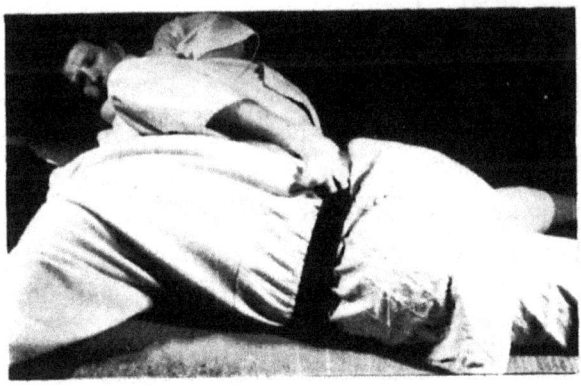

## 4. Hiza-gatame (Knee Holding)

Tori and Uke are facing each other in the Far Position. They come together, in Kyoshi, to the Near Position. From there they come slightly closer and hold each other in what may be called Right Kyoshi (i.e. with the right foot slightly forward, and holding opponent's left eri and right sleeve as in a standing Right Shizentai).

Tori releases his hold on Uke's right sleeve and passes his hand down and inwards, in a big circle, ending up by applying his left palm to the outside of Uke's right arm just above the elbow. The effect is to trap Uke's right wrist under Tori's left armpit.

With both hands he pulls Uke forward off balance, and puts his right toes against the top of Uke's left thigh by the groin. Falling backwards he applies his left toes to the side of Uke's back. The inside of his left knee comes on top of his left hand which is holding Uke's elbow, and now by twisting his hips to the right a lock comes on.

Uke tries to free himself by thrusting with his right palm, but failing to get his arm out gives the signal *Mairi*.

Tori releases the lock and withdraws to the Near Position. Uke rises and faces Tori in Kyoshi.

## Hiza-gatame (*Notes*)

The full name of this technique is Ude-hishigi Hiza-gatame.

It used to be done on the other side, because the Kyoshi itself was on the other side. Tori used to grip the sleeve at the end of his circling action, whereas now he applies the palm.

Uke has to be brought down on to Tori's right knee; Tori's left toes come near Uke's belt. Uke's body is controlled (*a*) by the trapped wrist, and (*b*) by Tori's right sole standing on and pushing at his left thigh (the push with the right foot is easier if it is made on the knee, but then the pushing leg loses much of its effectiveness in holding Uke because it becomes completely straightened; many teachers used to push at the middle of Uke's thigh, but it is now standardized as 'near the groin'), and (*c*) by Tori's right hand pulling Uke to him to stop a twist, and (*d*) Tori's left foot, on Uke's hip near the belt, which stops a somersault.

Uke's left knee used to be pushed away so that he came down on to his chest on the mats; the present directions leave it apparently optional whether Uke remains supported on his left knee (though bent right forward), or whether his left leg goes back so that it no longer supports him.

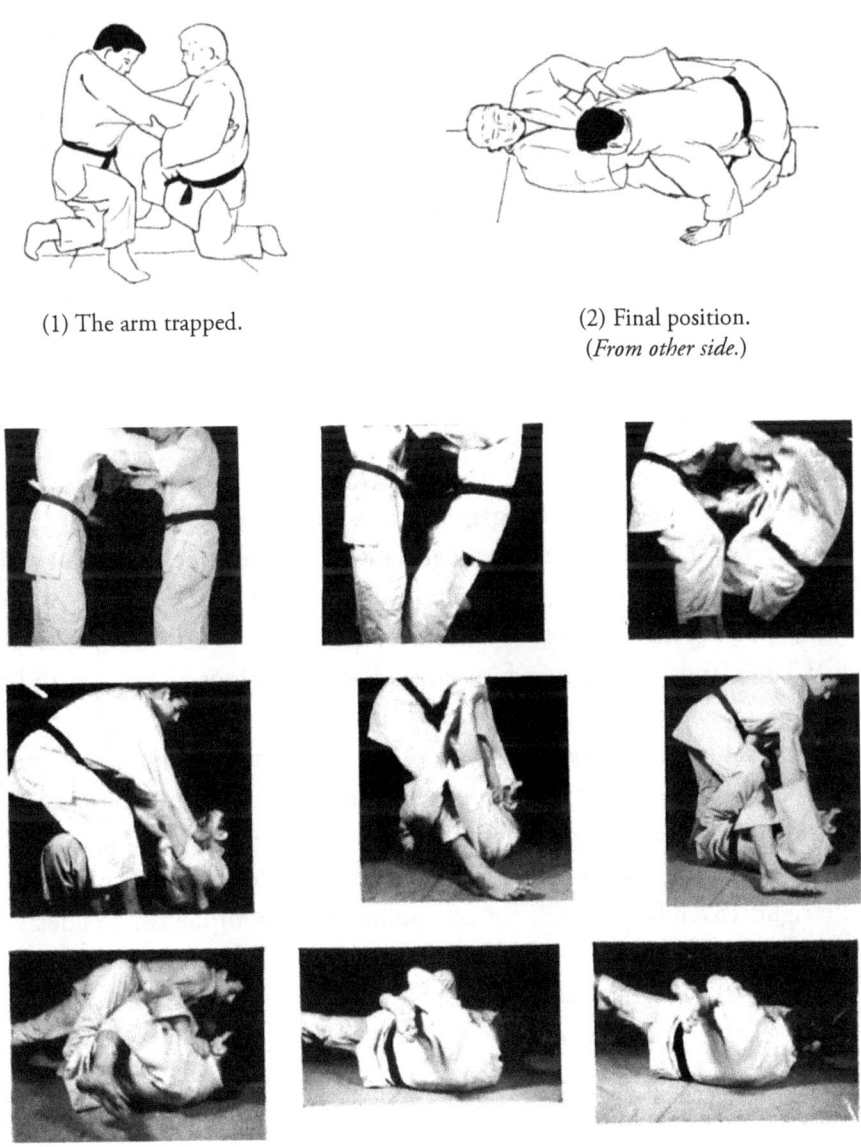

(1) The arm trapped.

(2) Final position.
(*From other side.*)

Note that Tori must get right under Uke when he makes the first attack with Tomoe, or he can never thread the leg through neatly. (From Joseki.)

135

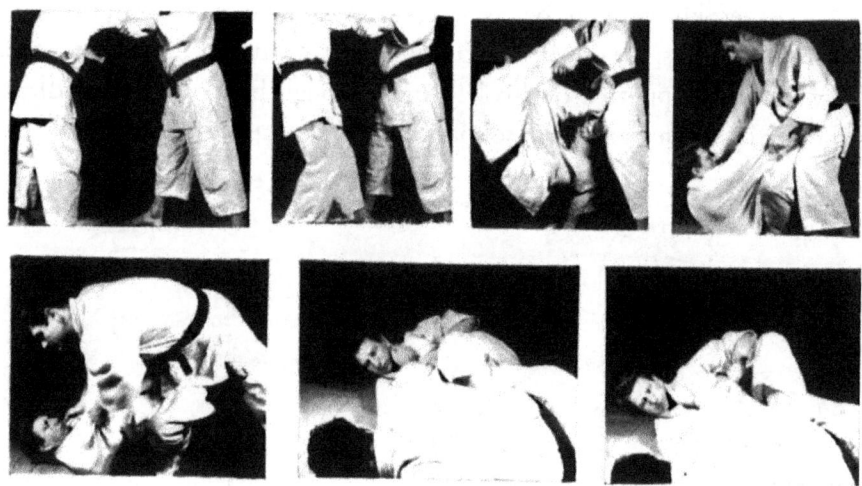

From opposite Joseki.

## 5. Ashi-garami (Leg Winding)

Tori and Uke stand up and engage in Right Shizentai.

Tori pulls Uke off balance to the front with both hands and steps in with his left foot between Uke's feet. He throws himself to the ground on his back, applying his right sole to Uke's lower abdomen in a Tomoe position.

Uke defends by stepping forward with his right foot and makes to lift Tori up. Tori uses this opportunity to get his hips in as far as possible, thrusts with his right foot against the inside of the opponent's left knee, and pulls him down to the front. His left foot goes through, behind and round to the outside of Uke's right leg, and finally the toes come right round and push in a wedge action against Uke's right abdomen, while Tori twists his hips to the right. Extending the left leg and pulling with both hands, he effects a lock on Uke's knee.

Uke tries to free himself by twisting his body to the left, but failing to escape gives the signal *Mairi*.

Tori releases the lock and both resume Kyoshi Position.

## Ashi-garami (*Notes*)

In the old style there was no attempt at Tomoe; Uke was simply pulled forward.

Special practice is necessary to get the winding leg well through.

Tori's right leg thrusts against Uke to make him lose balance forward, just as in Hiza-gatame, but now the thrust is made against the knee, whereas in Hiza-gatame it has been decided that it should come near the groin.

The hands must pull well in.

This is a difficult one to bring off well if you are tall, and you must practise again and again to get it neatly. If the legs are stiff it never looks well.

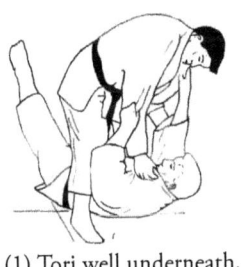

(1) Tori well underneath.

(2) Threading the leg through.

(3) Final position.

## Concluding moves.

Tori withdraws two steps to the Far Position and Uke withdraws one step to his original position, both still in Kyoshi, facing each other.

Tori and Uke stand up together, coming into Shizentai. Both take a step back (with the right foot first) and stand facing each other. Then they sit down in the formal position and exchange a formal bow in the sitting position. Coming upright again they face to the front and make the concluding standing bow to Joseki.

THE DEMONSTRATION OF GENTLENESS

# INTRODUCTION

J U-NO-KATA (formal demonstration of Ju or gentleness) was a special exercise for two people devised by Dr. Jigoro Kano, the founder of modern Judo. It requires no special clothing or equipment, and can be practised anywhere. As one of the leading figures in Japanese education early this century, Dr. Kano introduced Junokata into the physical education of Japanese youth, and it was and is widely practised in schools, especially by girls, to whom he believed it was specially suited. A knowledge of Junokata is now part of the syllabus for the Ladies' Section of the British Judo Association, which is thus continuing the tradition of Japan where some of the best exponents are women.

The word Ju, literally softness, has a technical meaning in Judo. The classical example is a willow which gives before the fury of the tempest, so that at the end its flexible branches remain unbroken, whereas the rigid oak is uprooted. Sometimes the principle is misunderstood as complete non-resistance. But it should be noted that the willow does use some strength, in that it keeps its root firm; it is only that it does not directly resist the force of the wind. Similarly, in Judo, force is not directly resisted: but there is indirect resistance. The indirect resistance is based on balance, skill and strategy.

Junokata combines several aims. It is a *physical culture* which develops a flexible all-round physique; it is a *physical education* in using the whole body with firmness and precision, and in the principles of disturbing and preserving balance; its *psychological interest* is profound because the movements are methods of nullifying force applied to the body; it develops *inner calm* because students have to learn mental poise while facing force or while being held.

*Physical Culture.* The stretching movements are carried to the limit; in particular Junokata makes the spine extremely flexible and also loosens the shoulders. In several of the movements the partner has to be lifted and held clear of the ground; when this is done skilfully the strong muscles of trunk and legs are exercised.

*Physical education.* The student learns to use the right amount of force in the right direction, and to use the body as a unit. Untrained people have their body-consciousness, motor and sensory, mainly in face and hands, the trunk being relatively undiscriminated. (Studies of cortical representation by Pen-field and others show this clearly.) Junokata training gives a much better awareness and control of the body as a whole.

Balance in most people is extremely poor: they try to align themselves in accordance with supposed vertical and horizontal lines in the objects around them. Experiments have been done in Japan in which a man tries to stand upright while a vertically striped 'tent' hangs round him; when the tent is revolved the untrained man invariably loses balance because the visual cues are disturbed, whereas the Judo men with their inner sense of balance can stand steadily even on one leg.

*Psychological interest.* Force applied against the body, and methods of evading it, excite the instinct of self-preservation, the most primitive of all. The interest aroused by Judo touches deeper levels than most sports, especially highly artificial games with complicated rules.

*Inner calm.* Most people, especially women, become confused if confronted with force or suddenly caught. In Junokata the applications of force are stylized representations of attacks with fist or stick, and so on, and the movements are generally practised slowly. Nevertheless, the escapes can be brought up to a speed at which they would be completely effective. From this point of view Junokata gives confidence and poise needed by nervous people.

## Practice

For a long time Junokata is practised slowly, in order to master the delicate manipulations of balance and force. Accuracy is aimed at from the beginning, and not too much energy is used. Gradually speed is increased and more force put in.

If it be objected that such methods of training are not those commonly adopted in most sports today, it can be replied that Junokata requires a very high degree of precision. If we consider activities where precision is required, like music or typewriting, or shorthand for that matter, we shall always find that accuracy is insisted on first of all, and then speed gradually increased. No musician would attempt practising fast passages on the principle that many mistakes are allowable at first and they can be ironed out later on. Experience shows that if speed is attempted too soon, precision is never in fact achieved.

Slow movement is not contrary to the spirit of Junokata. If the opponent's balance is correctly controlled, the movements will be effective even though performed quite slowly.

However, the Kata must not become 'dead'. The Kata is called dead when the movements are made mechanically and the performers forget the point of what they are doing. Traditional teachers had special ways of preventing it – during a slow movement the teacher would suddenly jump in and make a throw, taking the pupil aback. By these means the pupil was kept awake. The final aim is a calm alertness, without preconceived ideas or tensions but fully responsive to the whole situation.

To have done Randori or free practice is a great help to Kata, and Dr. Kano introduced Kata in most cases after some proficiency had been reached at Randori. However, the Junokata is specially designed so that it can also be practised with advantage by those who for any reason cannot undertake Randori.

Fig. 1

144

Fig. 2

*Technique*

Figures 1 and 2 show Dr. Kano performing two typical releases and counterattacks of the kind which come in Junokata. In Figure 1 notice the extended fingers, which are now about to grasp opponent's wrist. The latter's arm is twisted back into an awkward position, and he is *off balance* so that he has for the moment little mobility. This last point comes out even more clearly in the second picture, where the opponent's balance has been clearly broken to his rear. In both these pictures Dr. Kano is about to come forward to catch the opponent with his other hand and pull him still farther back.

For the Junokata moves to be effective, the opponent must be brought off balance so that his mobility is restricted, while you yourself must remain on balance with relatively free movement. If you get it right, you will be able to effect the moves without unnecessary force. *Some* force must be used: the aim of Judo is to use the right amount to attain the object, neither more nor less. It is a mistake to run through the Junokata simply in pantomime, as it were, with neither performer really affecting the other. There must be definite pushes, twists and pulls so that this Kata (like every other Kata) actually works. When performed well, Junokata can be very beautiful, but the beauty arises from economy and efficiency of movement directed to an end – it is not a series of poses meaningless in themselves.

On the other hand the moves should not be ponderous; the Kata must be dexterous. Judo techniques are designed to overcome even heavier and stronger opponents, and if the body is properly used they will come off neatly.

*Timing* is most important. The refinements are learned from a teacher, but they are developments of certain simple principles. Attacking force has to be avoided and deflected, so that the attacker's impetus carries him farther than he expected, and in a slightly different direction. This means that he begins to lose balance. As he loses balance, his effective strength becomes less, and this is the moment for the counter-movement to begin. In several of the Junokata sequences, the opponent manages to recover from the counter, and counters in his turn. The net result is to familiarize both partners with various stages of loss and recovery of balance, so that they can adapt themselves spontaneously and naturally to different physical situations.

A deeper subtlety is the use of opponent's reaction. Take, for instance, a typical sequence: A has momentarily the stronger balance and pushes at B. B has to give way but manages to adapt his posture so that he can develop resistance. When A feels what is happening, he gives a final push to bring B's resistance to the maximum, then suddenly stops pushing. B's resistance, now unopposed, brings him back in the opposite direction. A helps him along by a new movement, a pull. A and B are now exerting force on B's body in the same direction, and this is technically called 'Harmony'. The result is that B completely loses control.

Harmony results when A manoeuvres so that B reacts in a certain direction, and then A himself applies force on B in the same direction. There are other instances also in the Junokata. The harmony is not that of two friends cooperating towards the same end; A and B are co-operating, it is true, but under the ultimate control of A towards an end which B does not desire. The cooperation is that of master and slave, or trickster and his dupe. Of course, from the highest point of view, A and B are co-operating in the Kata, and B voluntarily assumes the role of loser. Thus on the highest level there is harmony in the true sense, harmony in training oneself and the partner, exemplifying Dr. Kano's principle: 'Mutual aid leading to mutual benefit.'

*Feeling,* of position and movement, must be developed in Junokata. If the body is hard, fine discriminations are impossible. Have a look at an expert musician or dancer; there is no unnecessary tension, yet the movements are made with firmness and precision. The word 'relaxation' gives most people the impression of floppiness, so it is a dangerous word to use; the secret of the Judo movement is a balancing of relaxation and tension. Hints can be taken from the movements of a cat; they cannot be called lacking in accuracy, yet somehow we feel they are relaxed. The point is that there is no unnecessary tension.

The ancient Chinese classic *Tao Te Ching* recommends us to look at the infant. The hand is soft and the muscles weak, yet its grip is firm. If we study how it holds, we find each little finger holding firmly; adults often try to use their hands as if they were rigid claws. As a result they do not conform to the shape of the thing held, and the grip is surprisingly easy to break.

Fig. 3

These are deep points, and they must be studied over a long period before we can expect to put them into practice. But they are very interesting.

Judo teachers with distinguished contest records study them, in the Katas including Junokata, and Dr. Kano himself said that this research is essential. The proper general handling of the body is one of the great things to be learnt from Judo, and when it is learnt we have a great advantage in mastering any other type of physical activity.

## Stylization

Look at Figure 3 on page 146. Here the man is extending his arm, which he takes round in a big circle, finally forming the hand into a fist and directing it at the opponent. This is the first move of one of the Junokata sequences. The preliminary action is, of course, quite artificial and would never precede any real blow. There are a number of such moves in Junokata, and some people wonder why they are there.

One purpose is to train what is called Nai-ki, or 'inner energy'. When making the big circle of the arm, draw in the breath and feel the energy running right down to the extended finger-tips till they tingle with it. Perhaps our present physiology has no satisfactory explanation as yet, but it is a fact that students who practise these methods do display exceptional energy and fine coordination even into old age. The subject deserves further investigation, but meantime the practice is there to be taken advantage of.

## Final Notes

In the descriptions which follow, *Uke* is the term for the one who initiates the first movement, and who finally ends up caught by the technique (*waza*) applied by the defender or *Tori*. All the sequences in Junokata are in fact counters, in the sense that one man initiates a movement of attack and this is ultimately turned to his disadvantage – though sometimes with several changes of fortune in between. The philosophy behind this construction of the Kata need not be explained here; it is enough to say that Dr. Kano believed that the ideal in life is to use skill to check and nullify force, and that the superior man does not resort to force except in defence.

Sometimes a sequence ends with Uke in the air. He gives the *Mairi* signal of submission ( a light double-beat with the hand on the body), because Tori could apply a decisive Judo throw. The throws are not carried out in

Junokata because that would involve going on the ground, necessitating special clothes, etc. Here I just show the actual throws for reference. Figures 4 and 5 illustrate *Ura-nage* or rear throw, in which the thrower goes down and pitches the opponent over the top on to his shoulder – a very heavy fall. In *Seoi-nage* (Figures 6 and 7) the opponent's arm is caught from below and he is pulled over Tori's back. In *Maki-komi* (Figure 8) the arm is caught from above and he is whirled over as the thrower himself goes down.

Joseki, from which position is calculated, is the place of honour in the Judo hall: it is generally the wall opposite the door.

The photos in this book, a unique series taken specially for instruction purposes, show Dr. Kano, the founder of Judo, himself performing the Junokata. These pictures were presented to the author in 1939 by the then President of the Kodokan, Jiro Nango, with instructions to use them for Judo in Britain. To carry out this request I have written this book around them.

I have not burdened the text by describing all that can be clearly seen from the pictures. Take the pictures as the basis, an authoritative demonstration by the genius who founded Judo: the text notes are merely supplementary.

In some places Dr. Kano had his demonstrations taken from a point other than Joseki: where this occurs I have put in drawings (for which I am grateful to Mr. T. Broadbent, 1st Dan) to show how the position looks from the normal angle.

T. P. LEGGETT,
RENSHUDEN JUDO CLUB.

Fig. 4 Uranage (1)

149

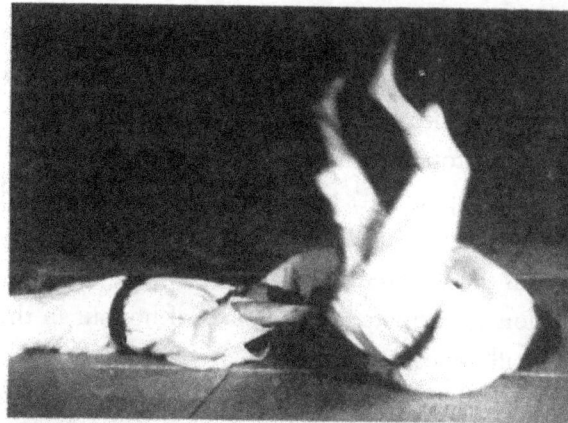

Fig. 5 Uranage (2)

Figs. 6 and 7 Seoinage

Fig. 8 Makikomi

## THE STANDING BOW

Tori and Uke stand about 8 feet apart, facing Joseki. They make a formal bow by sliding the extended fingers round the thighs till they touch the kneecaps. The eyes look down. The feet are rather close.

They turn to face each other and make the same bow.

Then they each step forward (right foot, left foot) to face each other with the feet under the shoulders.

# FIRST SECTION

## 1. Tsuki-Dashi (Forward Thrust)

(1) Uke (*on right*) and Tori are 6 feet apart. Note Dr. Kano's wonderful Shizenhontai posture in advanced age; few young men can stand so well. Even the famous teacher on the right does not achieve such a perfect natural upright posture.

(2) Uke advances in right Tsugiashi, i.e. with right foot always leading and the left foot being drawn up each time a half-step behind it.

(3) The thrust is at the point between the eyes.

(4) Tori steps to the side with his right foot and catches the outstretched wrist with his right hand, thumb down.

(5) Tori pulls Uke forward and up till he comes in front. He grasps Uke's left wrist with his own left hand, thumb up. Tori stretches Uke's body up and back; he does not bend his own knees.

(6) Uke frees his wrists by turning to the left and himself catches the wrists as they both turn.

(7) Uke turns Tori and brings him in front of him.

(8) This is the position of (5), but reversed. But note Uke holds with both his thumbs uppermost. Tori in (5) had his right thumb down.

(9) Tori executes a similar escape. Note the extended fingers of his left hand, and that Tori is turning to his right.

153

(10) Same as (5), but now Tori has both thumbs uppermost.

(11) Tori releases Uke's left wrist.

(12) And pulls his right arm straight up.

(13) Tori steps back a pace (left foot, right foot) and holds Uke helpless, bent back with his body extended and prevented from twisting out by the pull on his arm and Tori's left hand on his left shoulder.

Tori waits until Uke gives the *Mairi* signal of defeat by beating his body twice with the left hand, then returns Uke to the upright posture. Tori turns to the right and stands still; Uke moves to Tori's left back corner, ready for Kata-oshi, the next technique.

## 2. Kata-oshi (Shoulder Push)

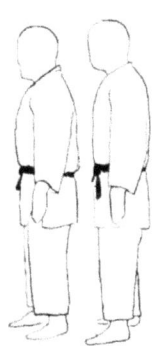

(1) Dr. Kano's photographer has moved to the point opposite Joseki, so that details of the movement show more clearly. The drawing shows Kata-oshi as it appears from Joseki.

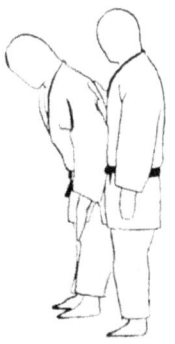

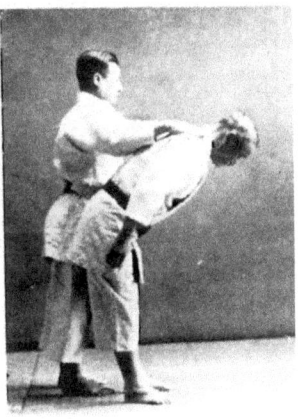

(2) Tori must keep legs straight as he yields to Uke's push.

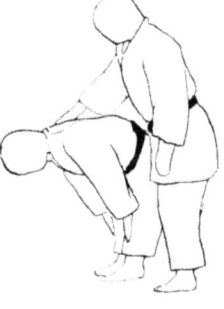

(3) Note that Tori's legs are still straight.

155

(4) Tori about to catch Uke's right hand, with his thumb in the centre of the palm. Uke is preparing to thrust at the point between the eyes with his extended left fingers.

(5) Uke tries to avoid the lock on his right arm by (*a*) the thrust and (*b*) by twisting. Tori catches Uke thrusting left hand similarly.

(6) Tori has stepped back a pace (right foot, left foot) and draws Uke's hands diagonally upwards, to get the maximum stretch on Uke's body.

Uke gives the *Mairi* signal by lightly stamping on the mat, and Tori returns him to the upright position, stepping forward a pace to do so. Tori stands still, and Uke stands about 2 feet away, facing him, in position for Ryote-dori

## 3. Ryote-dori (Double Wrist Grip)

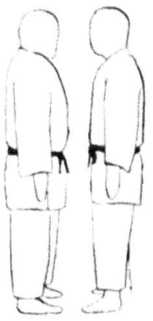  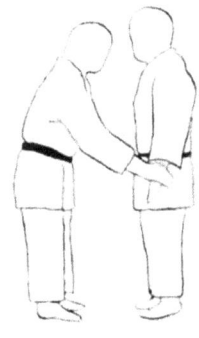

(1) To show the movement more clearly, Dr. Kano's photographer is again opposite Joseki. Uke grips both wrists. The drawing shows position seen from Joseki.

(2) Tori bends slightly forward.

(3) Tori releases right wrist by twisting in and up. Note extended fingers and slight twist of body.

(4) As seen *from* Joseki: Tori brings right arm over and releases left wrist by drawing it back. Note extended fingers preparing to grip Uke's right wrist.

(5) Tori has caught and drawn out Uke's left wrist and is preparing to lift Uke in a Makikomi action. Tori should ideally not grip the Judogi here or any time during Juno Kata. He just puts his arm round Uke's arm. Note Uke's left hand which helps him to keep balance in the slow motion.
(*For Makikomi, see the Final Notes of the Introduction.*)

(6) Uke arches his back at the end and straightens the ankles. Tori does not throw but when Uke gives the signal *Mairi* with the left hand Tori lowers Uke gently on to his feet again.

Tori stands still. Uke moves a little back, then approaches for the next movement.

## 4. Kata-mawashi (Shoulder Turning)

(1) Uke comes and stands about 1 foot behind Tori. He places his right hand on the top back of Tori's right shoulder, his left hand on the top front of the other shoulder (not yet applied in the photograph), and prepares to turn Tori round.

(2) Tori gives way by pivoting on his left foot.

(3) *{Taken from opposite side to show the action)* Tori's left hand slides down the inner sleeve (to grasp finally at the elbow).

(4) Tori comes through and grasps Uke's shoulder as high as possible, pulling him forward; note Tori's bent knees. Tori does not grip the Judogi— at least in ideal theory.

(5) Tori's left foot finishes level with his right. He holds Uke tightly to him and lifts him in Seoinage.

Uke points his feet and arches his back. His left hand rests on Tori's left hip, as in the Makikomi lift in Ryote-dori (p. 23).

Uke gives the *Mairi* signal with his left hand and Tori lowers him.

(*For Seoinage, see the Final Notes of the Introduction.*)

## 5. Ago-oshi (Chin Push)

(1) Tori faces Joseki and Uke stands something under 6 feet away. Note here Dr. Kano's perfect Shizenhontai, this time seen from the front.

(2) Uke advances in Tsugiashi (i.e. right foot always in the lead and left foot always at least half a pace behind) and raises the right arm as he advances.

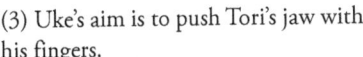

(3) Uke's aim is to push Tori's jaw with his fingers.

(4) When the hand is about to touch, Tori catches it with his right hand (thumb on the palm and pressing away and forward).

(5) Tori takes his right foot through in a very big arc, turning so that he twists Uke's right arm. Uke tries to relieve the pressure by turning to his right, supplementing this with a thrust of his left fingers towards the eyes.

(6) Tori catches the left hand in similar fashion as it comes through and makes Uke twist much farther than he intended.

(7) Uke pulls his arms in as they become fully extended, in order to avoid the finish of Kata-oshi. Tori complies by pushing Uke's hands to the top of his shoulders, but secures the same finish as regards spine and balance. Uke gives the *Mairi* signal with one foot, and Tori returns Uke to the upright position. Tori and Uke return to the positions in which they began the Kata, i.e. 6 feet apart.

# SECOND SECTION

## 1. Kiri-oroshi (Downward Cut)

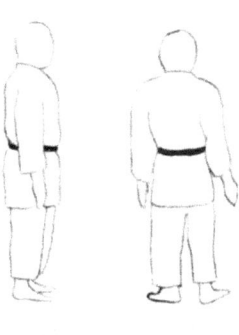

(1) Uke advances to face Tori about 3 feet apart. Uke pivots on his left foot and faces away from Joseki. *All the photographs except the last have been taken from opposite Joseki in order to show the movement;* the drawings show Kiri-oroshi as seen from Joseki.

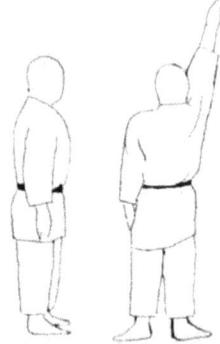

(2) Uke swings his right arm out to the side and straight up.

(3) Uke pivots on the left foot to turn to the left, and then advancing the right foot, strikes down at the head as if with a sword blade.

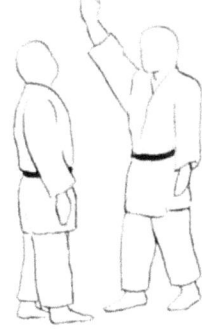

(4) Tori steps back (left foot, right foot) and the blow passes in front of him; he catches the hand as it passes.

(5) Tori takes a big step with the right foot and presses Uke's arm back and down. Note Tori's bent knees and wide stance.

(6) Tori draws up his left foot and again advances with the right; Uke steps back with his right foot, his arm fully extended. By keeping his balance Uke nullifies the effect of Tori's push, and Tori's own position becomes weak as he comes right in front of Uke.

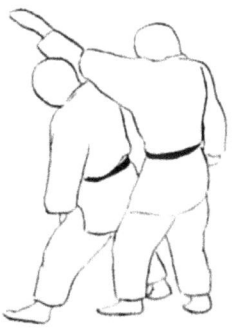

(7) Uke frees his right wrist from Tori's now weakened hold by turning his right thumb down and pushing Tori's elbow with the power of his body. His push begins to turn Tori.

(8) Tori continues to turn, moving his right foot in a big curve.

(9) Tori finishes his turn. Note how the right foot has travelled round; the left foot was the pivot.

(10) Tori straightens up and catches Uke's left wrist with his own left hand (thumb down).

(11) Tori moves right behind Uke (left foot, right foot) pulling Uke's arm to unbalance him to his left rear.

(12) Tori steps well back with the left foot and pulls Uke's arm up and out; his right hand goes up towards Uke's left shoulder.

(13) (*This picture is taken from Joseki*) Tori holds Uke off balance directly to the rear. Uke gives the *Mairi* signal with the right hand and Tori puts him back on balance.

Tori stands with Joseki on his left, in readiness for the next movement.

## 2. Ryo-kata-oshi (Double Shoulder Push)

(1) Uke moves to Shizenhontai about 2 feet behind Tori.

*(All photos except the last taken from opposite Joseki – the drawings are as seen from Joseki.)*

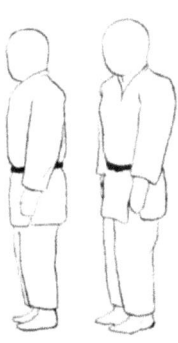

(2) Uke raises his hands, pointing the fingers and keeping the backs of the hands close to his chest . . .

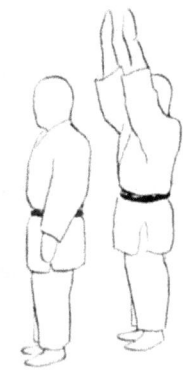

(3) . . . continuing 'till the arms are fully stretched. .

(4) He brings the hands down on to Tori's shoulders and presses down.

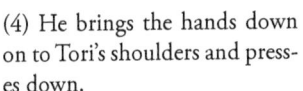

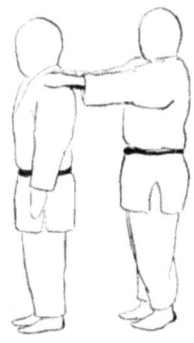

167

(5) Tori gives way

(6) . . . and turns in a series of small steps, beginning with the left foot.

(7) Tori has come round to face Uke. He holds the wrist . . .

(8) . . . and turns farther in the same way, pulling Uke forward.

c

(11) Rising a little, Tori goes forward with small steps, pulling Uke after him.

(12) To forestall any forward throw, Uke pushes at Tori's hips and pulls back.

(13) (After Tori has pulled Uke three or four steps altogether) Tori stops and utilizesnd Uke's resistance; Tori turns to throw off Uke's left hand . . .

(14) . . . and makes a big step with his left foot and then with the right foot, bringing him to Uke's right rear in Jigotai, knees bent. He has increased the pull on Uke's arm, and with his straight left arm he unbalances Uke to the rear, so that he could easily throw him down if necessary. Tori must show great firmness in the final pose.

Uke gives the *Mairi* signal with the left hand and Tori puts him back on balance.

### 3. Naname-uchi (Slanting Cut)

Uke comes to face Tori one step away (about 3 feet).

Uke raises his right hand, fingers extended, over his left shoulder. He brings the outside edge of the hand towards the point between Tori's eyebrows. Tori leans back to let the blow pass. With his left hand (fingers extended) he sweeps Uke's right hand out, controlling Uke's balance.

(1) Tori extends his right-hand fingers (separating middle and ring fingers a little) and thrusts at Uke's eyes.

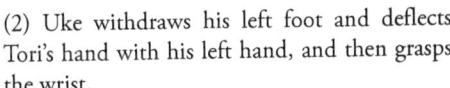
(2) Uke withdraws his left foot and deflects Tori's hand with his left hand, and then grasps the wrist.

(3) Tori steps forward with the left foot to recover his balance and releases Uke's right wrist. With his left hand (thumb below) he grips Uke's left wrist and pushes, so that he frees his right wrist and begins to take Uke off balance. Uke saves himself by applying his right palm (fingers pointing down) to Tori's left elbow. Uke begins to push Tori round in a curve.

(4) Uke has freed his left wrist by his push and is turning Tori, who begins to sink as he turns on his left foot.

(5) Tori passes right under Uke's right arm and takes his right foot behind Uke, coming against him so that the bodies form a T. Tori's right arm encircles Uke's hips and presses him against Tori's right hip. Tori's left hand comes on the left side of Uke's abdomen.

(6) Tori raises Uke by straightening his knees and pushing his hips forward. Uke is helpless against Ura-nage; he stretches his arms up and gives the *Mairi* signal by clapping his hands. Tori then sets him down.
(*For Uranage, see Final Notes in Introduction.*)

172

## 4. Kata-te-dori (One Hand Grip)

(1) Tori stands facing Joseki; Uke comes beside him. (Dr. Kano here faces slightly to one side of Joseki; however, most teachers face straight forward.)

(2) Uke grips Tori's wrist. Tori takes his arm forward and up. (Some teachers recommend a slight forward step with the right foot, and stretching the fingers.) Uke holds

(3) Tori has freed himself by bending his elbow, applying a lever action against Uke's arm. Uke brings up his right hand and pushes Tori's arm still farther, stepping forward to help his push. (Some teachers apply the left hand to Tori's left shoulder to pull him round.)

(4) Tori gives way and moves to the left, shifting his left foot, but twists the upper part of his body more than the lower, so creating an opportunity to slide in his left arm round Uke's waist along the belt-line. His right arm clasps Uke's left elbow to him.

(5) and (5A) Tori withdraws his right foot a trifle and lifts Uke with Uki-goshi. 5A shows the position from the opposite side. Uke holds his body in a straight line. Tori may take him up until the feet are well higher than the head.

Uke gives the *Mairi* signal with his right hand and Tori puts him back on his feet.

## 5. Kata-te-age (Arm Raising)

(1) Uke comes to face Tori and stands about 6 feet away. Uke and Tori simultaneously raise their right arms out to the side and then up, coming on to tiptoe.

(2) In little steps, at first slowly and then quickening, they come together; after three or four steps they meet at the right shoulder.

(3) Tori avoids a collision by quickly taking his right foot back and turning away. Uke, carried by his impetus, makes a big step with the right foot, coming in front of Tori. (Some teachers here recommend that Tori should bend his right knee.) Tori holds Uke to him with his left hand on top of the arm and pushes Uke down to his right. (Tori may hold Uke's right wrist to help the push.) Uke reacts back.

(4) Tori has suddenly released his pressure and changed to a push in the opposite direction. Tori is now pushing in the same direction in which Uke is trying to move, so that they are in what is technically called 'Harmony'.

(5) Uke again braces himself against this new attack by Tori; Tori again lets go so as to permit Uke to come upright. Note the hand position.

(6) As Uke comes up Tori shifts his right hand to Uke's wrist and pulls him out and up.

(7) Tori moves his left hand to the shoulder point and steps back (left foot, right foot) pulling Uke up and back till Uke is fully stretched out and completely off balance.

Uke gives the *Mairi* signal with the left hand and Tori returns him to the upright position.

Tori and Uke return to their original positions in which they began the Kata. This is the end of the Second Section.

# SECTION THREE

## 1. Obi-tori (Grasping the Belt)

(1) Uke comes to face Tori about 3 feet away. Uke raises his hands out and over . . .

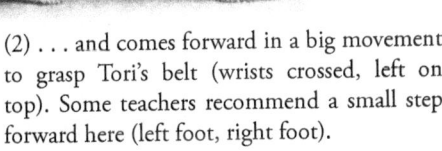

(2) . . . and comes forward in a big movement to grasp Tori's belt (wrists crossed, left on top). Some teachers recommend a small step forward here (left foot, right foot).

(3) Tori takes his hips slightly back and pulls aside Uke's left arm by applying his right palm to the wrist. Then Tori applies his left hand as shown, the inside edge against Uke's arm and the thumb separated. Tori may pivot on the left foot to help the movement.

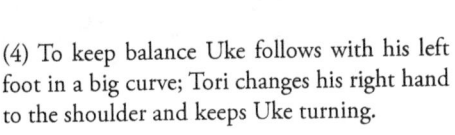

(4) To keep balance Uke follows with his left foot in a big curve; Tori changes his right hand to the shoulder and keeps Uke turning.

(5) As Uke comes right round he pulls at Tori's elbow and then moves his right foot back to complete his turn. (There is to be no break in the turning movement, however.)

(6) Tori has given way to the pull and made a half-turn by bringing his right foot through. Uke pulls at his left shoulder to unbalance him.

(7) Tori's feet stay almost as they are; he unexpectedly twists his upper body so that Uke's pull fails to unbalance him. He slides his left arm in for Ukigoshi.

(8) Tori holds Uke tightly against him . . .

(9) . . . and raises him in Ukigoshi. Some teachers take Uke's feet high. Uke should keep his body straight.

Uke gives the *Mairi* signal with his right hand and Tori sets him back on his feet.

## 2. Mune-oshi (Chest Push)

Uke comes to face Tori, and stands close to him.

(1) Uke raises his right hand, fingers straight, to shoulder level, takes his shoulder a bit back, and then pushes firmly at Tori's left chest.

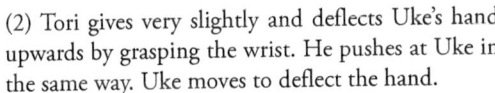

(2) Tori gives very slightly and deflects Uke's hand upwards by grasping the wrist. He pushes at Uke in the same way. Uke moves to deflect the hand.

(3) Uke carries Tori's right hand up, and gets his own right hand down to grip Tori's wrist.

(4) Tori grasps Uke's left wrist and lifts it firmly on high; then he takes his right foot back (and the left slightly forward if necessary), and moves his left arm down and through, carrying Uke's arm with it.

(5) Tori passes through with small steps, carrying Uke round with him. Note the extended fingers.

(6) Tori swings his left arm up and his right arm down, continuing to turn and taking Uke with him. The shoulders brush together all the time.

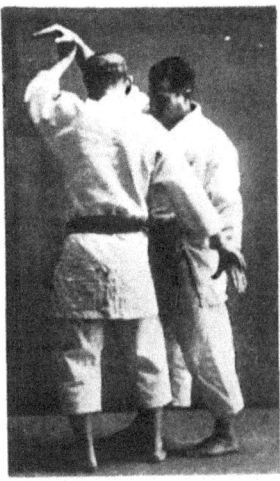

(7) A second half-turn almost complete, Tori frees his left wrist and grasps Uke's wrist.

(8) Tori pulls Uke's right arm straight out to the side and carries his left arm diagonally upward to the side. Releasing his right hand grip he slides the hand down Uke's arm. Uke begins to be bent over his right back corner.

(9) Tori takes a big step with his right foot, ending up with his hips behind Uke's. He bends his knees a trifle if necessary.

Uke is helplessly bent over and gives the *Mairi* signal with one foot. Tori sets him back on balance.

## 3. Tsuki-age (Upper Cut)

Uke comes to face Tori about 3 feet away.

(1) Uke takes his right foot back in a big step and swings his arm out, extending the fingers.

(2) and (2A) The arm fully stretched and the step complete.

(3) and (3A) Uke brings the hand down as a fist.

(4) and (4A) He steps forward with the right foot and directs the fist at Tori's jaw.

(5) Tori leans back a little, and if necessary takes a small step back, to make Uke miss; as the fist goes past he pushes it on its way with his right hand.

(6) Tori then brings up his left hand and pushes Uke's right elbow so that Uke begins to turn.

(7) Tori makes a big step to his left front; Uke turns on his left foot, taking his right through in a curve.

(8) Tori gives him no chance to recover balance but pulls his arm at the elbow and as Uke braces back (bringing his right foot forward now or a little later). . . .

(9) Tori threads his right arm through . . .

(10) . . . and steps right behind Uke, taking the hips through and lowering his body into Jigotai. Uke's arm is caught in Ude-garami.

(10A) The final position from the other side. Tori's right fingers rest on his other arm; his left hand is on Uke's forearm (it can be near the wrist).

Uke gives the *Mairi* signal with his free hand, and Tori releases him and puts him back on balance.

## 4. Uchi-oroshi (Downward Blow)

Uke faces Tori about 3 feet away.

(1) Uke takes his right hand diagonally across his body to the shoulder, slowly opening the fingers.

(2) and (2A) when the hand comes above the head the fingers are fully extended.

(3) The palm turns out as the hand swings away to the side.

(4) The arm comes down and the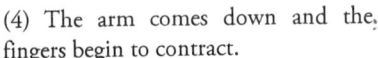 fingers begin to contract.

(5) The hand is brought up the front of the body, becoming a fist.

(6) Without a break in the smooth movement, Uke stretches his fist up . . .

(7) . . . and steps forward to bring the back of the knuckles on to Tori's head.

(8) Tori leans back (retreating a small step if necessary) so that Uke's fist misses and travels down; Tori establishes 'Harmony' by pushing Uke's arm further in the direction in which it is already going . . .

(9) . . . and takes a b;g forward step, pushing forward and down on Uke's wrist, making Uke withdraw his right foot to keep balance. (Some teachers make Tori move two or three small steps in the same direction before Uke adjusts his position.)

(10) When Tori's forward push is spent, Uke having successfully retained balance, Uke uses his left palm to turn Tori round by pushing the elbow, thus also freeing his own right wrist.

(11) Tori recovers and allows himself to be turned (note the raised arm in this and similar movements), pivoting on his left foot. Uke brings his right foot forward again.

(12) Tori slides his right foot in a very big curve, using Uke's own left arm as a connecting rod to unbalance him (a very fine point in this Kata, which has also important applications in Randori in the higher flights). Tori goes well down in Jigotai.

(13) Tori takes Uke's left wrist and keeping Uke tilted off balance, moves behind him (left foot, right foot).

(14) Tori has got right behind, and establishes a form of Hadakajime, his feet wide, knees bent and body turned rather to the left. He must keep Uke's body and arm extended, with a potential lock on the elbow.

Uke gives the *Mairi* signal and Tori puts him back on balance.

## 5. Ryo-gan-tsuki (Thrust Towards Eyes)

Uke comes to face Tori and stands about 3 feet away.

(1) Uke raises his right hand up his right side (palm down, fingers extended with middle and ring fingers a little apart). He takes his shoulder a little back.

(2) Uke steps forward and thrusts towards Tori's eyes. Tori avoids by stepping back with the left foot and turning out of the way. He grips Uke's wrist and carries the hand on, pulling Uke forward.

(3) Uke comes forward with the left foot and in his turn grips and pushes Tori's wrist, twisting his own right wrist free.

(4) Tori (shifting his left foot now or later to assure his balance) pushes with his right palm at Uke's elbow as it straightens out.

(5) Uke cannot maintain his hold, and is turned to the right, pivoting on the right foot.

(6) As Uke comes round, Tori thrusts towards his eyes, advancing the left foot slightly.

(7) Uke steps well back with the right foot, turns to the right and grasps the attacking wrist just as Tori did in (2).

(8) Tori recovers balance by advancing his right foot; he grips Uke's wrist to free his own left wrist.

(9) Uke in his turn pushes at the elbow and Tori begins to turn away, drawing in his left foot a little at the beginning but thereafter twisting mainly the shoulders and (ideally) without moving the feet more. As Uke turns Tori, he draws up his own right foot.

(10) Tori leans a little back and slipping under the arm moves into Ukigoshi; his foot movement should be minimal.

(11) Tori lifts Uke in Ukigoshi, Uke straightening out. The feet may be taken well up.

Uke gives the *Mairi* signal and Tori restores him to his feet.

### Conclusion of the Kata

Tori and Uke face each other 6 feet apart. They withdraw one step (the reverse of the step at the beginning of the Kata, left foot, right foot) bringing the feet close together, and make a standing bow. Then they turn towards Joseki and bow simultaneously.